Quick Vegetarian Curries

Quick Vegetarian Curries

Mridula Baljekar

Thorsons
An Imprint of HarperCollins*Publishers*

Thorsons
An Imprint of HarperCollins*Publishers*
77–85 Fulham Palace Road,
Hammersmith, London W6 8JB

Originally published as *Vegetarian Balti Cooking* by Thorsons, 1995
Published by Thorsons, 1999

10 9 8 7 6 5 4 3 2 1

Illustrations by Ken Cox

A catalogue record for this book is available from the British Library

ISBN 0 7225 3845 6

Printed and bound in Great Britain by
Woolnough Bookbinding Limited, Irthlingborough, Northamptonshire

In memory of my grandmother
who inspired me as a child.

Acknowledgements

I wish to thank KT Achaya, author of *Indian Food – A Historical Companion* which has been invaluable in collecting information about food, cooking utensils and crops in the Indus Valley Civilization. The book has also been very helpful in providing material about Kashmir and its food.

The Reader's Digest *Library of Modern Knowledge* has been an excellent source of information in compiling some of the historical facts.

Contents

Foreword

Certain types of food, and certain methods of cooking, are currently gathering momentum. Recent scientific discoveries have encouraged a global awareness towards vegetarianism. The World Health Organisation recently advised us to eat five types of fruits and vegetables every day. More and more natural foods are being produced and vegetarian menus in restaurants are becoming a common factor.

In India, however, vegetarianism has been a way of life for thousands of years. Although this was mainly due to religious beliefs, the findings of modern scientific research have strengthened the age-old practice of following a vegetarian diet. The message conveyed by this great momentum is simple: "you are what you eat". A vegetarian diet promotes a healthy body as well as a healthy mind.

I have never been a strict vegetarian myself, but having grown up in India, with its abundance of fresh vegetables, fruits, beans and pulses, eating meat has never been very important. We enjoyed eating meat and poultry dishes, but only in small quantities, along with generous helpings of vegetables, lentils, beans, salads etc.

The stressful pace of modern life also limits the time we would like to spend in the kitchen. Vegetarian food is not only quick to prepare and cook, but also very economical. It saves time and effort – you can easily rustle up a delicious meal even if you have not visited the shops for a few days. As long as you have a well stocked store cupboard with the basic spices and ingredients, like lentils and beans, a quick and easy meal is always at your fingertips.

I find the joy of cooking vegetarian meals simply irresistible! If you are a newly converted vegetarian, I am sure this book will offer you the inspiration to discover that vegetarian food can be delicious and exciting. For those of you who are established vegetarians, you will find a diverse range of nutritious recipes packed with flavour and taste.

With all my best wishes for a healthy body, mind and soul and a stress-free time in the kitchen.

Introduction

Electrical Tools

Modern technology offers every possible electrical gadget to make life easier in the kitchen. Take full advantage and make them work for you.

Make onion, ginger and garlic purée in a blender or food processor and store each one in small quantities. I keep these in a set of airtight containers in the fridge for frequent use. Use 1½ teaspoons of puréed garlic when a recipe calls for 3–4 cloves of garlic. Similarly, use 1½ teaspoons of puréed root ginger for a 2.5cm/1 inch cube. A little more or less garlic or ginger will not have a dramatic effect on your dishes.

Of course you can buy ginger and garlic purée ready to use, but they will not have the wonderful flavour which you get by making your own.

I also store a good quantity in small containers in the freezer.

You can chop fresh coriander (cilantro) in the food processor and freeze it in a freezer container. Break off small portions and use as required. Fresh green chillies can be frozen and used straight

from the freezer too. They will keep better if you freeze them with the stalks intact.

A coffee mill is essential for grinding dry spices.

If you have a pressure cooker, use it to cook lentils, dried beans and peas quickly and efficiently. These can be frozen and used for your chosen dishes as and when required.

Freezing Cooked Food

A majority of the dishes in this book will freeze successfully, as long as you are careful about what and how you freeze.

Vegetables such as potatoes (except when mashed), and to a certain extent aubergine (eggplant), do not freeze very well. Most other vegetables will freeze better if they are absolutely fresh when used.

All peas, beans and lentil dishes are excellent for freezing. Cooked rice dishes and all breads also freeze very well.

When cooking for the freezer, it is wise to undercook the vegetables slightly. Cool the dish quickly and chill before freezing. Spicy dishes taste even better when defrosted and reheated.

Always thaw the dish thoroughly before reheating. Do not panic if you find that your thawed dish has a lot of water content. This is because a certain amount of separation takes place when a dish is thawed. Do not attempt to drain it off, the vegetables will absorb all the water back into themselves during reheating.

When the dish is thawed and reheated, you may find that you need to adjust the salt and garam masala.

Here is a simple tip you can follow to give your defrosted dish an absolutely fresh appearance and flavour.

Heat about 2 teaspoons of cooking oil or ghee in a karahi or wok. Add ¼–½ teaspoon garam masala, depending on the amount of food you have, and a pinch of salt. Add the thawed dish and stir-fry until heated thoroughly, adding a little warm water if it becomes too dry. Stir in about 1 tablespoon of chopped fresh coriander (cilantro) leaves.

The dish will taste as fresh as if you have just cooked it!

Storing Indian Dishes in the Fridge

Indian dishes can be safely stored in the refrigerator for 3–4 days, sometimes longer. Indian spices have natural preserving qualities. So, when planning for a dinner party, you can cook ahead of time, reheat and present your food with absolute confidence.

Make sure the food is cold and put in an airtight container before storing in the fridge. Dishes containing acid ingredients like tomatoes, tomato purée (paste) and lemon juice will preserve the food for 48 hours, or longer, in perfect condition. Other dishes will keep well, though some vegetables may turn softer and the dish may look paler.

Follow the tips I have given for 'freshening up' frozen dishes.

How to Serve an Indian Meal

Traditionally Indian meals do not consist of several courses. Everything that is cooked for a particular meal, is generally put on the table for diners to help themselves as they wish. However, Western influence has changed this practice to a certain extent.

Starters are served in all Indian restaurants. It is entirely up to you as to what style you want to adopt, a traditional one or one that is influenced by Western culture.

Rice and bread are both served at dinner parties and large family gatherings. Generally, one starts off with bread with all the other dishes on offer and finishes with a little rice with the same curries.

Knives and forks are not normally used; you simply break off a small piece of bread and scoop up the curries with them, but many people prefer to use a fork or both spoon and fork to eat rice.

How to Store Spices and Prolong their Shelf Life

Whole spices have a much longer shelf life than ground. All spices, whole or ground, should be stored in airtight containers in a cool dark place. Ground spices lose their flavour very quickly even when they are stored properly.

The best way to preserve the flavour of spices is to heat them gently before storing. Simply preheat a heavy-based pan, add your chosen spice and stir until it releases its aroma. As soon as this happens (this usually takes about 1 minute), remove the pan from the heat and spread the spice on a large plate or tray.

Allow to cool thoroughly before storing in an airtight container. Ground spices treated this way will keep fresh for up to 12 months – whole spices even longer.

If you wish to buy whole spices and grind them yourself (this will always give you the best results) heat them gently as above, then cool and grind them. This heating not only enhances their flavour, but will also make them easier to grind.

Techniques of Cooking Spices

The secret of success lies in cooking and blending the spices correctly. The famous 'wet trinity' (onion, ginger and garlic) need specific cooking times with regulated heat to achieve the right flavours and textures. They also take much longer to cook than dry spices. Do not rush this stage and follow instructions carefully.

For cooking dry spices, always start on a medium or low-medium heat. Do not allow the oil to over-heat as the spices will burn quickly imparting an unpleasant, slightly bitter flavour to the dish. Spices need gentle heat to enhance their flavours. Overheating can cause them to lose their natural oils which impairs the flavours.

Using Salt

In Indian cooking, salt is used more as a spice rather than a seasoning agent. The quantity of salt used may appear excessive to the Western cook, but a certain minimum amount of salt is required to create a more balanced flavour of the spices. Without this, the dishes do not have the same authentic flavour. However, reducing salt in all food is essential to healthy living. Salt on its own is not the culprit, it is the sodium which causes concern. If you prefer, use low sodium salt, which is now readily available. You'll need to use a little more than normal salt.

Cooking and Serving Rice

Cooking rice to perfection is quite easy if you follow a few simple steps.

Before cooking: rice has quite a large amount of milling starch which you need to remove first. To do this, always wash the rice in several changes of water and soak it for 20–30 minutes then drain well. This process will not only remove much of the starch but will also enable the rice to absorb the water more easily during cooking, giving you perfectly fluffy, dry and separate grains.

During cooking: once you have put the lid on *never* be tempted to look at the rice. Leave it to cook for the specified time without lifting the lid or stirring it.

After cooking: remove the pan from the heat as soon as the rice is ready and keep it undisturbed for at least 10 minutes. Freshly cooked rice is rather fragile and allowing it to rest is very important. Fork through the rice and use a flat plastic or metal spoon to serve. Wooden ones tend to squash the grains.

Special Ingredients

The following is a list of the most commonly used ingredients in Indian and Pakistani cooking. You will also find hints about storing spices which require special care and attention.

Atta or chapatti flour: this is a very fine wholewheat flour used to make all Indian unleavened bread. It is rich in dietary fibre because unlike other wholemeal flour, atta is produced by grinding the whole wheat kernel to a very fine powder.

Ajowan or carum: ajowan is native to India and looks rather like a celery seed. It is related to caraway and cumin though in flavour it is more akin to thyme. All Indian grocers stock ajowan and the seeds will keep for a number of years if stored in an airtight container. Only tiny amounts are used in pulse dishes and fried snacks. Ajowan helps to prevent wind.

Bay leaf (tej patta): bay leaves used in Indian cooking are obtained from the cassia tree. They are quite different from Western bay leaves, which come from the sweet bay laurel. Indian bay leaves are rarely available in the West; standard bay leaves have become a popular substitute.

Black peppercorns (kali mirchi): fresh green berries are dried in the sun to obtain black pepper. The green berries come from the

pepper vine native to the monsoon forests of South West India. Whole peppercorns will keep well in an airtight jar while ground black pepper loses the wonderful aromatic flavour very quickly. It is best to store whole pepper in a pepper mill and grind it only when required. Pepper is believed to be a good remedy for flatulence.

Cardamom (elaichi): cardamom has been used in Indian cooking since ancient times. Southern India produces an abundance of cardamom from where it found its way to Europe through the Spice Route. There are two types of cardamom; the small green (choti elaichi) ones and the big dark brown (badi elaichi). In the West we also see a third variety. These are obtained by blanching the small green cardamom, and they have a milder flavour. Whole cardamom pods are used to flavour rice and different types of sauces. Ground cardamom, used in many desserts and drinks, can be bought from most Asian stores. It is best to grind small quantities at home using a coffee mill. Prolonged storage dries out the essential natural oils which destroys the flavour.

Cinnamon: cassia, used as cinnamon in Indian cooking, is one of the oldest spices. It is the dried bark of a tropical plant of the same name. Cinnamon is obtained from the dried bark of a tropical plant related to the laurel family. Cinnamon stick is indigenous to Sri Lanka which has complete monopoly. Cassia, on the other hand, grows all over the tropical countries. They produce similar flavours, but cinnamon is sweeter and more mellow.

Chillies (mirchi): it is difficult to judge the strength of chillies as different shapes and sizes will produce varying degrees of pungency. Generally, the small thin ones are hot and the large fleshy ones tend to be milder. Most of the heat comes from the seeds and to have a gentle kick without too much heat it is best to remove

them. One way to do this is to slit the chilli lengthwise into half and scrape the seeds away under running water. Use a small knife for this. Another way is to hold the chilli between your palms and roll it for a few seconds. This will loosen the seeds. You can then slit the chilli without cutting it through and simply shake out the seeds. The following types are normally used in Indian cooking:

Fresh green chillies (hari mirchi): the long slim fresh green Indian chillies are sold in Indian stores. Similar looking ones are sometimes sold in local greengrocers but these are usually from the Canary Islands and tend to be much milder than the Indian chillies.

Jalapeño and serrano chillies: from Mexico, these chillies are more easily available from supermarkets. Although these are not ideal for Indian cooking, they can be used when a recipe calls for fresh green chillies to be chopped or ground with other ingredients. When they are intended to be left whole, the long Indian variety look more attractive.

Dried red chillies (lal mirchi): when green chillies are ripe, their colour changes to a rich red. These are then dried to obtain dried red chillies. One cannot be substituted for the other as the flavour, when the chilli is dried, changes completely. The dried red 'Bird's eye' chillies which are small and pointed, are extremely hot and these are normally used whole to flavour the cooking oil. Long slim ones are much weaker and are used ground with other spices. Dried red chillies are ground to a fine powder to make chilli powder. Crushed dried chillies are obtained by grinding dried red chillies to a medium-coarse texture.

Cloves (lavang): cloves are unopened dried buds of a Southern Asian evergreen tree. They have a strong distinctive flavour and are

used both whole and ground. In India cloves are used as a breath freshener, and clove oil is used to remedy toothache.

Coconut (nariyal): coconut palms grow in abundance in Southern India. Fresh coconut is used in both sweet and savoury dishes. In the West, convenient alternatives are desiccated coconut, creamed coconut and coconut milk powder.

Coriander (cilantro), fresh (hara dhaniya): a much-used herb in Indian cooking, the fresh leaves of the coriander (cilantro) plant are used for flavouring as well as garnishing. They also form the basis of many chutneys and pastes. The fruit produced by the mature coriander (cilantro) plant is the seed which is used as a spice, and from which fresh coriander (cilantro) is grown.

Coriander (cilantro), seeds (dhaniya): this is one of the most important ingredients in Indian cooking. The sweet mellow flavour blends very well with vegetables.

Cumin seeds (jeera): like many spices cumin can be used either whole or ground. It is powerfully pungent and the whole seeds are used to flavour the oil before the vegetables are cooked in it. A more rounded flavour is obtained if the seeds are roasted and then ground. Because of their strength, they need to be used in measured quantities. There are two varieties, black (kala jeera) and white (safed jeera). Each has its own distinct flavour and one cannot be substituted for the other. Black cumin is sometimes confused with caraway.

Curry leaf (kari patta): grown extensively in the foothills of the Himalayas, these have quite an assertive flavour. Sold fresh and dried by Indian grocers, they are used to flavour vegetables and pulses. Dried curry leaves should be stored in an airtight jar and the fresh ones, which have a better flavour, can be frozen and used as required.

Dhanna-jeera powder: this is simply a mixture of coriander (cilantro) and cumin seeds which are ground together. The mix produces a different flavour from using ground coriander and cumin individually. This is because when the seeds in dhanna-jeera powder are mixed and ground together their natural oils combine at the same time. If you cannot get the mix, you can make your own by using 60 per cent coriander (cilantro) seeds and 40 per cent cumin seeds.

Dried fenugreek (Kasoori methi): a strong and aromatic herb characteristic of Northern Indian and Pakistani cuisines. It is native to the Mediterranean region and is cultivated in India and Pakistan. Both the seeds and leaves (fresh and dried) are used in cooking.

Fennel seeds (saunf): these greenish-yellow seeds, slightly bigger than cumin, have a taste similar to anise. They have been used in Indian cooking since ancient times. In India, fennel is used as a breath freshener. The seeds are also chewed to settle an upset stomach.

Garam masala: the main ingredients of garam masala are cinnamon or cassia, cardamom, cloves and black pepper. Other spices are added to these, according to preference. Though garam masala is available in the shops, it is easy to make your own (see the recipe on page 22).

Garlic (lasoon): fresh garlic is indispensable to Indian cooking. Dried flakes, powder and garlic salt cannot create the same authentic flavour. Garlic is always used crushed or puréed as these two methods produce more flavour. Garlic is beneficial in reducing the level of cholesterol in the blood and its antiseptic properties aid the digestive system.

Ghee (clarified butter): ghee has a rich and distinctive flavour and is used liberally in Mogul food. There are two types of ghee,

pure butterfat ghee and vegetable ghee. Butterfat ghee is made from unsalted butter and vegetable ghee from vegetable shortening. Ghee can be heated to a high temperature without burning. Both types of ghee are available from Indian stores and vegetable ghee is sold by some supermarkets. It is simple to make your own ghee (see page 21).

Ginger (adrak): fresh root ginger which has a warm woody aroma, is vital to Indian cooking. Dried, powdered ginger cannot produce an authentic flavour. Ginger is believed to improve circulation of the blood and reduce acidity in the stomach.

Mint (pudina): mint is native to Mediterranean and Western Asian countries. It is easy to grow and also available in most supermarkets. Dried mint, however, is a good substitute. Bottled mint sauce, which has a lovely fresh aroma, works very well in many recipes.

Mustard seeds (sarsoon or rai): these are an essential ingredient in vegetarian cooking. Out of the three types, black and brown mustard seeds are commonly used in Indian cooking, and lend a nutty flavour to a dish. White mustard seeds are reserved for making pickles, and the green leaves are used as a vegetable.

Nutmeg (jaiphal): the nutmeg plant is unique as it produces two fruits in one; nutmeg and mace (javitri). Nutmeg has a hard dark brown shell with a lacy covering. This covering is mace which is highly aromatic. It is removed from the nutmeg before being sold. The best way to buy nutmeg is whole. Pre-ground nutmeg loses the lovely aromatic flavour quickly. Special nutmeg graters are available with a compartment to store whole nutmegs.

Onion (pyaz): this is one of the oldest flavouring ingredients and rarely is any Indian cooking done without it. Brown, red and snow

white onions are grown and used extensively; the use of shallots and spring onions is also quite common.

Onion seeds (kalonji): these tiny black seeds are not produced by the onion plant. They are referred to thus because they have a striking resemblance to the onion seeds. Kalonji, available from Indian stores, are used whole for flavouring vegetables and pickles and to flavour Indian breads.

Paneer: paneer is often referred to as 'cottage cheese' in India, but it is quite different from Western cottage cheese. The only Western cheese which resembles paneer in taste, is ricotta, but, ricotta cheese cannot withstand the cooking temperatures that paneer can. Paneer is made by separating the whey from the milk solids and is an excellent source of protein. It is available from Asian stores or you can make your own (see pages 24–5).

Paprika: Hungary and Spain produce a mild sweet strain of pepper. Dried and powdered, this is known as paprika. 'Deghi Mirchi', grown extensively in Kashmir is the main plant which is used for making Indian paprika. It is a mild chilli pepper which tints the dishes with a brilliant red colour without making them excessively hot.

Poppy seeds (khus khus): the opium poppy, grown mainly in the tropics, produces the best poppy seeds. There are two varieties, white and black, but only the white seeds are used in Indian recipes. They are either ground, or roasted and ground, and help to give a nutty flavour to most sauces while also acting as a thickening agent.

Rose water: a special edible rose is grown in many parts of the country. The petals are used for garnishing Moghul dishes. They can also be crushed to extract their essence. This is diluted to make rose water which is utilised in savoury and sweet dishes.

Saffron (kesar): the saffron crocus grows extensively in Kashmir. Close to 250,000 stamens of this crocus are needed to produce just 450g (1lb) of saffron. It is a highly concentrated ingredient and only minute quantities are required to flavour any dish.

Shahi jeera (royal cumin): this is different from the normal cumin, and is sometimes known as black cumin seeds. It is a rare variety and, in India, grows mainly in Kashmir. It is also more expensive but its delicate and distinctive flavour is well worth the extra expense. The seeds will keep well almost indefinitely if stored in airtight jars.

Sesame seeds (til): these pale creamy seeds, with a rich and nutty flavour are indigenous to India. They are the most important of all the oil seeds grown in the world and India is the largest exporter of sesame oil to the West. The seeds are sprinkled over naan before baking, and are also used in some sweets and vegetables. They are an effective thickening agent for sauces.

Tamarind (imli): resembling pea pods when tender, tamarind turns dark brown with a thin hard outer shell when ripe. Chocolate brown flesh is encased in the shell which needs to be seeded before use. The required quantity of the flesh is soaked in hot water, made into a pulp and used in several dishes. These days, life is made easier by the availability of ready-to-use concentrated tamarind pulp. Lentils, peas, vegetables and chutneys benefit from its distinctive tangy flavour.

Turmeric (haldi): fresh turmeric rhizomes are dried and ground to give a rich yellow powder. India produces the largest amounts of turmeric. The quantity used in dishes has to be just right to prevent a bitter taste.

Vanilla: second only to saffron in terms of plant-to-shop costs, vanilla pods retain their flavour for years. They are usually stored

embedded in sugar. The sugar, now with a strong vanilla flavour, can be used in desserts. Vanilla essence is an effective alternative.

Yogurt (dahi): made with fresh whole milk, yogurt in India is almost always home-made. A mild flavour combined with a creamy texture it is a very useful ingredient in many dishes.

Basic
Recipes

Ghee

Melt 450g/1lb/2 cups unsalted butter over low heat and allow it to bubble gently. At this stage, you will hear a gentle splattering which is the moisture in the butter being driven off. After a while, the splattering will stop, indicating that most of the moisture has evaporated. Continue to heat the butter until the liquid is a clear golden colour and you can see the sediment (milk solids) at the bottom of the pan. This process can take up to 45 minutes depending on the quantity of butter you are using. Once the liquid and milk solids have separated, cool the butter slightly and strain it into a storage jar through a fine muslin. Ghee can be stored at room temperature. Vegetable ghee can be made the same way using margarine made of vegetable oils.

Garam Masala V

Makes 75g/3oz

The word 'garam' means 'heat' and 'masala' is a mixture of spices used to create a special flavour. Garam masala is made by blending together a few specially chosen spices for which the recipe can vary from one region or one cook to another. However, the basic spices which are known to create body heat remain the same, i.e. cassia bark or cinnamon stick, cloves and cardamom. To these basic spices you can add other ingredients like black peppercorns, cumin and nutmeg.

25g/1oz cassia bark or cinnamon sticks
25g/1oz whole green cardamom pods
15g/½oz whole cloves
8 bay leaves, broken up
2 teaspoons black peppercorns
3 whole nutmeg, crushed
3 teaspoons black cumin seeds

1. Preheat a small, heavy pan over medium heat for 2–3 minutes. When hot, reduce the heat to low and add the cassia or cinnamon and cardamom pods. Stir and roast for 1 minute.

2. Add the cloves, bay leaves, peppercorns and nutmeg, stir and roast for 1½ minutes.
3. Remove the pan from heat and add the black cumin seeds. Your pan will still be hot enough to roast the seeds, stir and roast them for 1 minute.
4. Allow the spices to cool thoroughly, then grind in batches until fine in a coffee grinder. Mix the batches thoroughly and store in an airtight jar. This will remain fresh for 10–12 months.

Paneer

Makes 225g/8oz

Paneer is an Indian home-made cheese which is now being made commercially. You can buy paneer from Asian grocers and good supermarkets. It is a very versatile cheese and is full of all the goodness of protein and calcium. To the large vegetarian population of India, paneer provides as much protein as meat, poultry and fish. If you wish to make your own, you will be delighted to see from the recipe below how easy it is to make. Unlike any other cheese, paneer needs no curing or maturing, which puts it in a class of its own.

2.6 litres/4½ pints/1⅓ cups full cream milk
125ml/¼ pint/⅔ cup lemon juice

1. Heat the milk in a heavy-based saucepan, stirring frequently to prevent it sticking to the bottom of the pan.
2. When the milk begins to rise, add the lemon juice and let it boil until the whey is separated from the curdled milk. This will become obvious in a minute or two when the milk becomes watery and the cheese floats to the top.
3. Strain the curdled milk through a fine muslin and tie up the ends loosely, leaving the cheese solids intact.

4. Hang the cloth in a cool place for 1 hour to allow all the water to drain off.
5. You can convert the paneer into a block by placing a weight on top. Hang the muslin for 5–10 minutes only, then roughly shape the paneer into a block, leaving it in the cloth, and place a weight on top. Leave for 2–3 hours. Remove from the muslin and cut into cubes.

Starters and Appetizers

A mouth-watering choice of starters and appetizers are included in this chapter. These are also very versatile: you can serve some of them with drinks, or as side dishes; some can form a light meal. In every case, instructions are provided for different ways of serving them.

Shakahari Shamee Kabab

(Vegetarian Shamee Kabab)

Makes 12

Shamee Kabab is Mogul in origin and the Moguls, being Muslims, are basically meat eaters. I have created this vegetarian version using potato and paneer, the Indian cheese. Do make sure that you peel the potatoes after boiling, rather than before, to avoid any stickiness. You can serve these with a relish and bread for a main meal too.

2 large slices white bread (about 100g/4oz)
375g/13oz/2¼ cups potatoes, boiled, peeled and mashed
200g/7oz/1 cup paneer, grated or mashed
1–2 green chillies, seeded and finely chopped
2–3 cloves garlic, peeled and crushed
½ teaspoon chilli powder (optional)
1 teaspoon salt or to taste
15g/½oz/¼ cup finely chopped coriander (cilantro) leaves
1 small onion (about 100g/4oz/1 cup), finely chopped
or minced
25g/1oz/⅕ cup plain flour, seasoned
1 large egg, beaten
Oil for shallow frying

1. Lay the slices of bread side by side on a large plate and pour over enough cold water to soak them for a few seconds. Hold the bread, one slice at a time, crumpled between your palms and squeeze out all the water. Put in a large mixing bowl.
2. Add the remaining ingredients except the flour, egg and oil. Using a potato masher, mash the ingredients until thoroughly blended together. Alternatively, put all the ingredients (except the onion, flour, egg and oil) in a food processor and blend until smooth. Add the onions and mix.
3. Divide the mixture into 2 equal parts and make 6 equal-sized balls from each. Flatten the balls into smooth round cakes.
4. Put enough oil in a frying pan to measure about 5mm/¼ inch depth and heat over medium heat. Dust each kabab in the seasoned flour, making sure it is fully coated. Dip the kababs in the beaten egg and fry until well browned on both sides. Drain on absorbent paper.

Preparation time: 25 minutes
Cooking time: 10–12 minutes
Serving ideas: Serve with a raita.
Variation: Use Cyprus halloumi cheese, but reduce the salt as halloumi is already salted.

Suran Pakoras V

(Spiced Yam Slices)

Serves 6–8

Suran or yam is also known as elephant yam and its use in Indian cooking dates back to the Aryan times. The Aryan civilization consisted of Nomadic tribes.

If you have not cooked or eaten yam before, try this delicious spicy recipe. You can buy yam in good supermarkets and Asian stores.

900g/2lb/6½ cups yam
1 teaspoon salt or to taste
1 teaspoon ground turmeric
1–1½ teaspoons chilli powder
1 teaspoon ajowan (carum) seeds
25g/1oz/⅕ cup besan (gram flour), sifted
15g/½oz/⅙ cup ground rice
Oil for deep frying

1. Peel the yam and cut into 5mm/¼ inch thick slices. As yam has rather thin ends and is quite thick in the middle, cut the bigger slices in half. Soak the slices in cold water for 30 minutes, then drain but do not dry them.

2. Put the salt, turmeric, chilli powder, ajowan seeds, besan and ground rice in a large mixing bowl and mix well. Add the yam slices and mix until they are fully coated with the spiced besan.
3. Heat the oil for deep frying in a wok or other suitable pan over medium-high heat. Fry the yam slices in batches in a single layer for 3–4 minutes or until they are crisp and golden brown. Drain on absorbent paper.

Preparation time: 15 minutes, plus 30 minutes to soak the yam
Cooking time: 12–15 minutes
Serving ideas: Serve with drinks or as a starter with Pudina aur Hara Dhaniya ki Chutney (pages 173–4) or as a side dish with rice and a lentil dish.

Paneer Sashlik [V]

(Indian Cheese Kababs)

Serves 6

Here is a wonderful vegetarian version of the well-known tandoori dish. Instead of lamb or chicken, you can use that versatile Indian cheese, paneer, to make these scrumptious kababs. If you cannot get or make paneer, use tofu or Cyprus halloumi cheese. Reduce the quantity of salt if you use halloumi. For a quick and filling meal, serve these wrapped in a naan or roti.

2 tablespoons lime juice
4 cloves garlic, peeled and crushed to a fine pulp
1 teaspoon ground coriander
1 teaspoon ground cumin
½ teaspoon ground turmeric
¼–½ teaspoon chilli powder
½ teaspoon Garam Masala (pages 22–3)
1 teaspoon salt or to taste
3 tablespoons sunflower or corn oil
200g/7oz/1 cup paneer, cut into 2.5cm/1 inch cubes
75g/3oz/⅔ cup red pepper, cut into 2.5cm/1 inch cubes
75g/3oz/⅔ cup green pepper, cut into 2.5cm/1 inch cubes

100g/4oz/1 cup closed cup mushrooms, halved, or small whole button mushrooms
150g/5oz/1¼ cups red onions, peeled and cut to the same size as the mushrooms
40g/1½oz/⅕ cup butter, melted for basting

1. Mix together all the ingredients up to and including the oil in a small bowl.
2. Put the paneer, peppers, cauliflower, mushrooms and onions in a large mixing bowl. Pour the marinade over, then stir and mix thoroughly. Cover and leave to marinate for 3–4 hours, or overnight in the fridge. Remove from the fridge 30 minutes before cooking.
3. Preheat the grill to medium, line a grill pan with foil and lightly brush with oil.
4. Thread the marinated paneer and the vegetables onto individual skewers, alternating them evenly. The onion pieces will separate when cut, just put together several pieces to make one chunky piece.
5. Place the skewered kababs on the prepared grill pan and brush over any remaining marinade. Place the tray about 10cm/4 inches below the grill and cook for 2–3 minutes. Brush with melted butter and cook for a further 2 minutes. Turn the skewers over and brush with the remaining melted butter, then cook for a further 4–5 minutes and remove.

Preparation time: 20–25 minutes, plus marinating
Cooking time: 10 minutes

Serving ideas: Serve with any naan accompanied by Ghia ka Raita (pages 168–9).

What to do with leftovers: Cook Kesari Chawal (pages 144–5), heat the paneer and vegetables by tossing them in a non-stick pan over a medium heat for a few minutes. Mix with the rice to make a delicious cheese and vegetable pulao.

Gobi Pakoras V

(Spiced Cauliflower Fritters)

Serves 4–6

Patoras can be made from any vegetable. Here, cauliflower is just an example. You could use broccoli, aubergine (eggplant) or green peppers cut into chunks.

1 cauliflower (about 375g/13oz/3¼ cups when outer leaves removed)
1 onion (about 175g/6oz/1½ cups), roughly chopped
1cm/½ inch cube root ginger, peeled and roughly chopped
4 cloves garlic, peeled and roughly chopped
2 green chillies, seeded
15g/½oz/¼ cup coriander (cilantro) leaves, including tender stalks, roughly chopped
150ml/¼ pint/⅔ cup water
200g/7oz/1½ cups besan (gram flour), sifted
75g/3oz/½ cup ground rice
1¼ teaspoons salt or to taste
½ teaspoon chilli powder (optional)
½ teaspoon ground turmeric
75ml/3 fl oz/⅓ cup water
Oil for deep frying

1. Divide the cauliflower into 2.5cm/1 inch florets.
2. Put the onion, ginger, garlic, chillies and coriander (cilantro) leaves in a blender. Add the first measure of water and blend until smooth.
3. In a large mixing bowl, mix the besan, ground rice, salt, chilli powder (if used) and turmeric. Add the blended ingredients and remaining water and mix to a thick batter.
4. Heat the oil in a wok or other suitable pan over a medium heat. The temperature of the oil should be about 160°C. Drop a tiny amount of the batter, about the size of a lemon pip, into the oil. If it surfaces immediately without browning, the oil is at the right temperature.
5. Increase the heat slightly and dip each cauliflower floret in the batter, making sure it is fully coated.
6. Fry as many pakoras as you can in a single layer without over-crowding the pan. Each batch will take 6–7 minutes to brown, turn them over once or twice. Drain on absorbent paper.

Preparation time: 15 minutes
Cooking time: 15–20 minutes
Serving ideas: Serve as a starter with Pudina aur Hara Dhaniya ki Chutney (pages 173–4) or Ghia ki Chutney (pages 168–9). They are wonderful with drinks too! For a main meal, serve with naan or rice and a lentil dish.
Suitable for freezing.

Tala hua Palak V

(Batter Fried Spinach Leaves)

Serves 4

This was my mother's subtle way of making us eat spinach. She would pick large spinach leaves from the garden in the morning and serve them up for lunch, coated in a spicy batter and deep fried – totally irresistible!

12 large spinach leaves
90g/3oz/¾ cup besan (gram flour)
40g/1½oz/¼ cup ground rice
½ teaspoon ground turmeric
½ teaspoon chilli powder
1 teaspoon cumin seeds
1 teaspoon onion seeds (kalonji)
½ teaspoon salt or to taste
175ml/6 fl oz/⅔ cup water
Oil for deep frying

1. Wash the spinach leaves carefully without damaging them. Keep a 2.5cm/1 inch stem on each leaf. Dry thoroughly on absorbent paper.

2. Sift the besan into a large mixing bowl and add the remaining ingredients except the water and oil. Mix the dry ingredients well, then gradually add water, mixing until you have a thick batter.
3. Heat the oil in a wok or other suitable pan over medium-high heat. To check that the oil is at the right temperature, drop a tiny piece of the batter in the hot oil. If it surfaces immediately without browning, then the temperature is just right. If you have a thermometer, make sure that the oil is at least 180°C.
4. Hold each leaf by its stem and dip it in the batter, making sure it is fully coated. The stem should also be coated with the batter. Fry 2–3 leaves at a time, depending on the size of your pan. Cook until golden brown and crisp, this will only take 1–1½ minutes per batch. Drain on absorbent paper and serve immediately.

Preparation time: 15 minutes
Cooking time: 6–8 minutes
Serving ideas: Serve as a starter with Pudina aur Hara Dhaniya ki Chutney (pages 173–4).
Not suitable for freezing.

Palak Pakoras [V]

(Deep Fried Spinach Balls)

Makes 24

I am always surprised when I come across people who dismiss spinach as uninteresting and tasteless. For me, spinach is one of the most wonderful vegetables, offering complete flexibility in the way it can be cooked. Even if you are generally not interested in spinach, just try this recipe once, you'll love it! For deep fried snacks such as pakoras and bhajiyas which are coated with besan, the temperature of the oil is very important. You need to fry them gently to ensure that the inside cooks well and the outside browns gradually giving it a crisp texture.

155g/5oz besan/1 cup (gram flour)
60g/2oz/⅓ cup ground rice
1 teaspoon salt or to taste
¼–½ teaspoon chilli powder (optional)
1 teaspoon ground cumin
2 teaspoons ground coriander
1 teaspoon ground turmeric
½ teaspoon ajowan seed (carum)
1–2 green chillies, seeded and finely chopped
150g/5oz/2½ spinach leaves, finely chopped

150g/5oz/1¼ cups onions, chopped
150ml/¼ pint/⅔ cup water
Oil for deep frying

1. Sift the besan into a large mixing bowl and add the remaining ingredients except the water and oil.
2. Mix together, then gradually add the water until you have a thick paste-like consistency. Make 24 walnut-sized balls, to make this easier, divide the mixture into 4 equal parts and make 6 balls from each part.
3. Heat the oil in a wok or other suitable pan over medium heat. Check the temperature with a thermometer, if you have one, and ensure that it is at 160°C–170°C. If you do not have a thermometer, take a tiny amount (about the size of a pea) of the paste, without the vegetables, and drop it in the oil. If it surfaces immediately without browning, then the temperature is just right.
4. Fry the pakoras in a single layer in batches for 8–10 minutes, turning them over occasionally. Drain on absorbent paper.

Preparation time: 15–20 minutes
Cooking time: 20–25 minutes
Serving ideas: Serve as a starter with Ghia ki Chutney (pages 166–7). They are lovely with drinks too.
Suitable for freezing. Thaw and reheat under a preheated medium grill for 5–6 minutes, turning over half way through. Place the grill 15–25cm/6–8 inches away from heat.
Variation: Use methi leaves (fenugreek) instead of spinach.

Aloo Chaat

(Potato Relish)

Serves 4–6

Aloo Chaat is a famous North Indian appetizer. It is eaten cold and has a tangy, slightly hot flavour. Served sprinkled with Delhi or Bombay Mix, it makes a mouth-watering snack. If you cut the potatoes very finely, you can serve them on small savoury biscuits. Any left-overs are ideal for this. The tangy flavour comes from tamarind which is available in Asian shops. If you cannot get it use lemon juice, but the flavour will be different.

700g/1½lb/5 cups old potatoes
2 tablespoons chopped coriander (cilantro) leaves
2 tablespoons mint leaves or 1 teaspoon bottled mint sauce
1 green chilli, seeded and chopped
¼–½ teaspoon chilli powder (optional)
1 teaspoon salt or to taste
1¼ teaspoons tamarind concentrate or 2 tablespoons lemon juice
2 tablespoons water
1 small red onion, finely chopped

To garnish:

Bombay or Delhi Mix

1. Boil the potatoes in their skins, drain and cool thoroughly. Peel and dice into 1cm/½ inch pieces.
2. Put the remaining ingredients, except the onion, in a blender and blend until smooth. Pour this mixture over the potatoes and add the onion. Mix thoroughly.
3. Put into individual serving dishes and top with Bombay or Delhi Mix.

Preparation time: 20 minutes
Cooking time: 25–30 minutes

Shakurkandi Pakoras V

(Sweet Potato Fritters)

Serves 4—6

Sweet potatoes are readily available in most supermarkets. They can be stored and peeled just like ordinary potatoes. Cooked in a spicy batter, they produce a wonderful contrast of flavours and textures. The batter is made of besan which is also known as gram flour. You can buy it from Indian grocers, good supermarkets and health food shops. The temperature of the oil is crucial in frying pakoras successfully. Too low a temperature will result in soggy pakoras. If the temperature is too high, it will brown quickly, leaving the inside raw.

450g/1lb/3 cups sweet potatoes
175g/6oz/1¼ cups besan (gram flour)
75g/3oz/½ cup ground rice
1 teaspoon salt or to taste
1 teaspoon ajowan (carum) seeds
1 teaspoon crushed dried chillies
1 teaspoon ground turmeric
1 tablespoon ground cumin
15g/½oz/¼ cup fresh coriander (cilantro) leaves, including tender stalks, finely chopped

300ml/½ pint /1⅓ cups water
Oil for deep frying

1. Peel the sweet potatoes. Working from both ends, cut as many 5mm/¼ inch thick slices as possible. When the diameter of the slices gets bigger, cut the potato into half, lengthwise, and slice each half as before. Cut exceptionally large slices into quarters. You will have a few uneven shapes and sizes because of the varied sizes that sweet potatoes come in. Soak the sliced potatoes in salted water for 15 minutes, then drain and rinse.
2. Sift the besan into a medium-sized mixing bowl. Add the remaining ingredients except the coriander (cilantro), water and oil. Mix thoroughly with a wooden spoon, then add the coriander (cilantro) and gradually add the water while you continue to mix. Make sure the batter is smooth. When all the water is added, you should have a smooth, thick batter.
3. Heat oil in a karahi, wok or other deep frying pan over medium heat. If you have a thermometer, check that the temperature of oil is 160°C–170°C. If you do not have a thermometer, drop a small portion (about the size of a pea) of the batter in the oil. If it floats to the surface straightaway without browning, then the temperature is right.
4. Dip each slice of potato in the batter making sure it is fully coated, and shake off any excess batter back into the bowl. Fry as many slices as you can manage in a single layer without overcrowding the pan. Cook until evenly browned on both sides, turning over at least twice. Each batch will take 5–6 minutes. Drain on absorbent paper.

Preparation time: 20 minutes
Cooking time: 20–25 minutes
Serving ideas: Serve with a relish as a starter or with drinks.
Alternatively, serve as a side dish with any curry and rice.

Masaledar Badam Aur Kaju

(Spiced Almonds and Cashew Nuts)

Serves 6–8

Serve these deliciously spiced nuts with pre-dinner drinks, especially at Christmas time, with Spicy Pineapple Drink (see page 198).

1 large clove garlic, peeled and roughly chopped
1 teaspoon salt or to taste
125g/4oz/1 cup whole almonds
125g/4oz/1 cup raw cashew nuts
4 tablespoons water
1½ teaspoons chilli powder or to taste
2 teaspoons ground coriander
1 teaspoon ground cumin
25g/1oz/¼ cup besan (gram flour) sieved
Oil for deep drying

1. Crush the garlic and salt together to a fine pulp.
2. Put the nuts in a mixing bowl and add the remaining ingredients except the oil. Mix until the nuts are evenly coated.
3. Heat the oil over medium heat in a wok or other suitable pan for deep frying. When hot, but not smoking, fry the nuts for

6–8 minutes or until they begin to crackle gently. Drain on absorbent paper and serve when completely cold.

Preparation time: 10 minutes
Cooking time: 6–8 minutes

Vegetables

Fresh vegetables are important to us whether we are vegetarian or not. They provide essential vitamins and minerals, and cooking them the Indian way further enhances their natural values.

For example, garlic reduces the level of cholesterol in the blood and has antiseptic properties which aid the digestive system. Ginger is beneficial in reducing acidity in the stomach.

From the wide selection of recipes in this chapter, you will see how wonderful and interesting vegetables can be. Do try the unusual ones too; clear instructions for cooking and preparing have been given for all of them.

Paneer Makhani

(Indian Cheese in a Spicy Butter Sauce)

Serves 4

Paneer is packed with essential nutrients. To the vast majority of the Indian population it provides as much protein as meat and poultry.

225g/8oz/1 cup paneer or Cyprus halloumi cheese;
cut into 2.5cm/1 inch cubes
2 tablespoons sunflower or soya oil
4 green cardamon pods, bruised
2 x 2.5cm/1 inch pieces of cinnamon sticks
4 cloves garlic, peeled and crushed
2.5cm/½ inch cube of root ginger, peeled and finely grated
1 medium onion (175g/6oz/⅔ cup), finely chopped
2 teaspoons ground coriander
½ teaspoon ground turmeric
½ teaspoon chilli powder
65g/2½oz/⅓ cup butter
1 teaspoon salt or to taste
½ teaspoon sugar
150ml/¾ pint/⅔ cup passata or sieved canned tomatoes
150ml/¼ pint/⅔ cup single cream

3–4 green chillies (long slim variety) with the stalks intact
½ teaspoon Garam Masala (pages 22–3)
2 tablespoons chopped coriander (cilantro) leaves

1. Bring a panful of water to the boil and add the cubes of paneer. Bring back to the boil and let it cook for 1 minute, then drain. This prepares the paneer to absorb the flavours.
2. Place a heavy-based non-stick frying pan over a low heat and add the oil. Add the cardamon and cinnamon and allow to sizzle for 15–20 seconds.
3. Add the garlic, ginger and onion. Increase the heat to medium and stir-fry for 6–7 minutes or until the onion is soft with a light brown tinge.
4. Add the coriander, turmeric and chilli powder. Reduce the heat to low and cook for 1 minute, then add the butter, salt, sugar, passata or sieved tomatoes and simmer for 2–3 minutes.
5. Add the cream and paneer; simmer for 5 minutes and add the chillies, Garam Masala and coriander (cilantro) leaves. Simmer for 2–3 minutes, remove from the heat and serve.

Preparation time: 15 minutes
Cooking time: 20 minutes
Serving ideas: Serve with Kesari Chawal (pages 144–5).
Cook's Notes: If using halloumi, reduce the quantity of salt to half.
Not suitable for freezing.

Gobi Andey

(Cauliflower with Eggs)

Serves 4

An unusual and delicious way to serve cauliflower, this recipe is from my mother's repertoire. Not only does it taste good, it is also packed with protein and vitamins.

- 3 tablespoons sunflower or corn oil
- 1 teaspoon cumin seeds
- 1 teaspoon coriander seeds, pounded to a medium coarse texture
- ½ teaspoon onion seeds (kalonji)
- 1 onion (about 175g/6oz/1½ cups), finely sliced
- 1–2 green chillies, seeded and cut into juliennes
- ¼–½ teaspoon crushed dried red chillies
- ½ teaspoon ground turmeric
- 1 medium cauliflower, 500g/1lb/4 cups when outer leaves removed, cut into 2.5cm/1 inch florets
- ½ teaspoon salt or to taste
- 2 tablespoons chopped coriander (cilantro) leaves
- 4 medium eggs, lightly beaten

1. Heat the oil in a skillet or saute pan over a medium heat. When hot but not smoking, add the cumin and coriander, followed by the onion seeds.
2. Add the onion and green chillies. Increase the heat slightly and fry for 4–5 minutes. Add the red chillies and turmeric and fry for 1 minute.
3. Add the cauliflower and fry for 3–4 minutes. Stir in the salt, stir and reduce the heat to low. Cover the pan with a lid, and cook for 10–12 minutes. By this time the cauliflower should be tender but still firm, with all the natural juices in the pan.
4. Stir in the coriander (cilantro) leaves and increase the heat to medium. Pour the beaten eggs evenly over the cauliflower, allow to set for 1 minute, then stir until the eggs coat the cauliflower. Remove from the heat and serve.

Preparation time: 15 minutes
Cooking time: 20 minutes
Serving ideas: Serve with Tarka Dhal (pages 111–12) and Sada Chawal (pages 142–3). A raita is an optional extra.
Variation: Use broccoli instead of cauliflower.

Mattar-Paneer

(Peas with Indian Cheese)

Serves 4–6

Mattar-Paneer is a very popular dish in Northern India, especially in the state of Punjab. Use tofu or Cyprus halloumi cheese if you cannot find (or make) paneer.

4 tablespoons sunflower or corn oil
250g/8oz/1 cup paneer, cut into 2.5cm/1 inch cubes
1 teaspoon shahi jeera (royal cumin)
1 onion (about 175g/6oz/1½ cups), finely chopped
5–6 cloves garlic, peeled and crushed
2.5cm/1 inch cube root ginger, peeled and finely grated
2 teaspoons ground coriander
1½ teaspoons ground cumin
½ teaspoon ground turmeric
½ teaspoon chilli powder
1 tablespoon tomato purée (paste)
250g/8oz/1⅔ cups frozen garden peas, thawed, or cooked fresh peas
300ml/½ pint/1⅓ cups warm water
75g/3oz/½ cup canned chopped tomatoes
1 teaspoon salt or to taste

150ml/¼ pint/⅔ cup single cream
3–4 green chillies
2 tablespoons chopped coriander (cilantro) leaves

1. Heat the oil in a non-stick saucepan over a medium heat. When hot but not smoking, stir-fry the paneer cubes until golden brown. (Take care while frying paneer, as the oil tends to splatter quite a bit.) Drain on absorbent paper.
2. Allow the oil to cool slightly, removing the pan from the heat if necessary. Add the shahi jeera and stir-fry for 15 seconds. Add the onion and fry for 5–7 minutes. Stir frequently.
3. Add the garlic, ginger, coriander and cumin, reduce the heat slightly and fry for 1 minute. Add 2 tablespoons water and fry until the water evaporates. Stir constantly.
4. Add the turmeric and chilli powder and fry for 30 seconds. Add 2 tablespoons water and fry again until the water evaporates.
5. Add the tomato purée (paste), fry for 30 seconds, then add the peas and water. Bring to the boil, reduce the heat to low and simmer for 5 minutes.
6. Add the fried paneer, tomatoes, salt, cream and chillies. Increase the heat slightly and cook for 5 minutes. Stir in the coriander (cilantro) leaves and remove from the heat.

Preparation time: 15–20 minutes

Cooking time: 30 minutes

Serving ideas: Serve with Kesari Chawal (pages 144–5) or Peshawari Naan (pages 155–7), accompanied by a raita. If you do not have the time to make your own naan, you can use ready-made naans. Reheat under the grill, sprinkled generously with water, to keep them soft and fluffy.

Saag-Aloo

(Spinach with Potatoes)

Serves 4–6

Spinach leaves collected straight from the garden, glistening with morning dew, is one of my early childhood memories. If you do not have time to prepare fresh spinach which needs thorough cleaning and washing, you can use frozen leaf spinach, but not the purée.

- 375g/13oz/2⅔ cups old potatoes, peeled, cut into 5cm/2 inch cubes and boiled
- 3 tablespoons sunflower or corn oil
- ½ teaspoon black mustard seeds
- ½ teaspoon cumin seeds
- ¼–½ teaspoon crushed dried chillies
- 8 cloves garlic, peeled and crushed
- 1 onion (about 175g/6oz/1½ cups), finely sliced
- 1½ teaspoons ground cumin
- ½ teaspoon ground turmeric
- 275g/10oz/5 cups spinach, finely chopped
- 1 teaspoon salt or to taste
- 150g/5oz/⅔ cup canned chopped tomatoes, including juice
- ½ teaspoon Garam Masala (pages 22–3)
- 1 tablespoon tomato purée (paste)

1. In a sauté pan, heat the oil over a medium heat. When hot but not smoking, add the mustard seeds and as soon as they pop, add the cumin, crushed chillies and garlic. Stir-fry for 30 seconds.
2. Add the onion and fry for 6–7 minutes or until soft and just beginning to colour. Stir frequently.
3. Add the cumin and turmeric, and fry for 1 minute. Add the spinach and salt, and cook until the spinach has shrunk to half the original amount (about 3–4 minutes). Stir frequently.
4. Add the tomatoes, potatoes, garam masala and tomato purée (paste). Increase the heat slightly and cook for 2–3 minutes, stirring frequently, then remove from the heat and serve.

Preparation time: 25 minutes
Cooking time: 15 minutes
Serving ideas: Serve with Peshawari Naan or Sada Chawal (pages 155–7) and Dhal Makhani (pages 113–14).
Suitable for freezing before adding the potatoes; add them during reheating.
What to do with leftovers: If you have any leftover dhal, mix it with your leftover Saag-Aloo to create a wholesome new dish. Simply heat about 2 teaspoons of oil in a saucepan, add ¼ teaspoon Garam Masala (pages 22–3), then add your leftovers and stir-fry until heated through.

Bandhgobi Bhaji V

(Dry Spiced Cabbage)

Serves 4–6

A delicious way to cook cabbage – the spicing is subtle and the cabbage is cooked in its own juices. Do try and use red onion as it looks attractive and adds a distinctive flavour.

3 tablespoons sunflower or corn oil
1 teaspoon cumin seeds
1 onion (preferably red), finely sliced
6 cloves garlic, peeled and crushed
1 green chilli, seeded and cut into juliennes
¼ teaspoon ground turmeric
500g/1¼lb/9 cups green cabbage, finely shredded
1 teaspoon salt or to taste
1 tablespoon chopped coriander (cilantro) leaves

1. In a sauté pan or any shallow pan, heat the oil over a medium heat. When hot but not smoking, add the cumin seeds.
2. Add the onion, garlic and chilli. Stir-fry for 4 minutes and add turmeric. Stir fry for 30 seconds.
3. Add the cabbage and salt, fry for 2 minutes then reduce the heat to low. Cover the pan with a lid, and cook the cabbage in

its own juices for 10–12 minutes. If you like the cabbage really soft, cook for 15 minutes. Stir in the coriander (cilantro) leaves, remove from the heat and serve.

Preparation time: 20 minutes
Cooking time: 20–25 minutes
Serving ideas: Serve with Kashmir ki Roti (pages 150–1) accompanied by any dhal and a raita.
Suitable for freezing.
Variation: Use 2.5cm/1 inch cauliflower florets instead of cabbage.

Palak Paneer

(Spinach with Indian Cheese)

Serves 4

This is one of those all-in-one dishes which provides you with protein, carbohydrate, vitamins and minerals. Paneer is easy to make at home (see pages 24–5) but if you do not have the time, you can buy it from good supermarkets and Asian shops.

4 tablespoons sunflower or corn oil
250g/8oz/1 cup paneer, cut into 1cm/½ inch cubes
6 cloves garlic, peeled and crushed
1 small onion (about 100g/4oz/1 cup), very finely chopped
2.5cm/1 inch cube root ginger, peeled and finely grated
1 tablespoon ground coriander
1 teaspoon ground cumin
100g/4oz/½ cup canned chopped tomatoes including juice
½ teaspoon ground turmeric
1 teaspoon paprika
¼–½ teaspoon chilli powder
150g/5oz/2½ cups spinach, finely chopped, or frozen leaf spinach
300ml/½ pint/1⅓ cups warm water
175g/6oz/1¼ cups boiled potatoes, cut into 2.5cm/1 inch cubes
1 teaspoon salt or to taste

½ teaspoon Garam Masala (pages 22–3)
4 tablespoons single cream

1. In a saucepan heat 2 tablespoons of the oil over a medium heat. When hot but not smoking, fry the cubes of paneer until lightly browned, tossing and turning them constantly. This will only take 1½–2 minutes. Drain on absorbent paper.
2. Add the remaining oil to the pan and reduce the heat. Add the garlic and stir-fry for 1 minute, then add the onion and increase the heat to medium. Fry for 5–6 minutes, until softened.
3. Add the ginger, ground coriander and cumin, cook for 1 minute and add the tomatoes. Stir and fry for 3–4 minutes or until the oil floats on top.
4. Add the turmeric, paprika and chilli powder and cook for 30 seconds. Add the spinach and stir-fry for 2–3 minutes, then add half the water. Cook for 3 minutes or until the water dries up, tossing and turning the ingredients constantly.
5. Add the fried paneer, potatoes, salt and remaining water. Cook for 1 minute, then reduce the heat to low and simmer for 5 minutes, uncovered. Add a little more water if necessary.
6. Sprinkle on the garam masala, stir in the cream, remove from the heat and serve.

Preparation time: 25–30 minutes
Cooking time: 20 minutes
Serving ideas: Serve with Peshawari Naan (pages 155–7) and a raita.
Suitable for freezing (the texture of the cooked potatoes will change when thawed).

Variations: Use frozen garden peas instead of spinach, thaw them first. Fresh peas are lovely and should be cooked before adding to the sauce.

Use tofu or Cyprus halloumi cheese instead of paneer.

Bhindi Mirchiwali V

(Okra with Peppers)

Serves 4

A light and aromatic dish with an attractive appearance. The soft green colour of the okra contrasts beautifully with the bright red sweet pepper and sliced onions, and the entire combination in a little creamy sauce looks stunning.

225g/8oz/2⅔ cups bhindi (okra)
1 red pepper (about 150g/5oz/1¼ cups)
1 onion (about 175g/6oz/1½ cups)
1 tablespoon white poppy seeds
1 tablespoon sesame seeds
1 long slim dried red chilli, chopped
3 tablespoons sunflower or corn oil
4–5 cloves garlic, peeled and crushed
½ teaspoon salt or to taste
75ml/3 fl oz/⅓ cup warm water

1. Scrub each okra gently, rinse well in running water, then slice off the hard head.
2. Halve the pepper and remove the seeds and white pith. Cut into 4cm/1½ inch strips.

3. Peel and halve the onion lengthwise, then cut into 5mm/¼inch thick slices.
4. Grind the poppy seeds, sesame seeds and red chilli in a coffee grinder until fine.
5. Preheat a sauté pan or wok over medium heat and add the oil. When hot but not smoking, stir-fry the garlic for 30 seconds or until beginning to brown.
6. Add the onion and stir-fry for 2–3 minutes, then add the ground ingredients. Stir-fry for 30 seconds.
7. Add the okra and salt, stir-fry for 30 seconds and add the water. Reduce the heat to low, cover the pan with a lid, and cook for 5 minutes.
8. Stir in the red pepper, cover again and cook for 4–5 minutes. Remove from the heat and serve.

Preparation time: 20–25 minutes
Cooking time: 15 minutes
Serving ideas: Serve with Sada Chawal (pages 142–3) accompanied by Dhal Makhani (pages 113–14). Ghia ka Raita (pages 168–9) makes a good optional side dish.
Suitable for freezing.
Variation: Use whole green beans instead of okra.

Bandhgobi aur Moong Dhal Jhal Frazi

(Stir-fried Cabbage with Lentils)

Serves 4–6

Moong dhal is one of the fastest cooking lentils and it has a delicious earthy flavour. All Asian stores and some health food shops stock moong dhal. It is also known as yellow split lentils. Jhal frazi is akin to stir-frying and is, therefore, very quick.

4 tablespoons sunflower or corn oil
1 large onion (about 225g/8oz/2 cups), finely chopped
1 teaspoon shahi jeera (royal cumin)
6 cloves garlic, peeled and crushed
1cm/½ inch cube root ginger, peeled and grated
2 red chillies, seeded and chopped
100g/4oz/½ cup moong dhal, picked over, washed and soaked for 30 minutes, drained
½ teaspoon ground turmeric
300ml/½ pint/1⅓ cups warm water
350g/12oz/6 cups green cabbage, finely shredded
1 teaspoon salt or to taste
1 teaspoon ground cumin
2 tablespoons chopped coriander (cilantro) leaves

1. Heat the oil in a sauté pan or wok over a medium heat for 1–2 minutes. When hot, stir-fry the onion for 8–10 minutes golden brown. Tilt the pan and squeeze out as much oil as possible from the onion by pressing onto the side with a spoon. Drain on absorbent paper.
2. Reduce the heat slightly, and fry the shahi jeera in the remaining oil for 15 seconds.
3. Add the garlic, ginger and fresh chilli. Stir-fry for 30 seconds and add the drained dhal. Stir-fry for 1½ minutes, reduce heat to low and stir-fry for a further 1½ minutes.
4. Add the ground turmeric, stir-fry for 30 seconds, then add the water and half the fried onions. Increase the heat to medium and cook for 5 minutes, stirring frequently.
5. Add the cabbage and salt and stir-fry for 5 minutes.
6. Add the cumin, stir-fry for 2 minutes then add the coriander (cilantro). Stir-fry for 1 minute and remove from the heat. Serve garnished with the remaining fried onions.

Preparation time: 15–20 minutes, plus soaking dhal
Cooking time: 25 minutes
Serving ideas: Serve with Family Naan (pages 152–4) and a raita or chutney.
Suitable for freezing.

Shalgam ka Salan

(Spiced Turnips)

Serves 4–6

In this superbly flavoured dish, turnips are first fried in ghee then simmered gently in a spice-laced yogurt sauce which complements the natural flavour of the vegetable beautifully.

700g/1½lb/5 cups turnips, trimmed, peeled and cut into 4cm/1½ inch chunks
175g/6oz/1 cup thick set whole milk natural yogurt
2 teaspoons besan (gram flour)
50g/2oz/¼ cup ghee
1 teaspoon shahi jeera (royal cumin)
2 whole cloves
1 onion (about 175g/6oz/1½ cups) finely sliced
1cm/½ inch cube root ginger, peeled and cut into juliennes
2 teaspoons ground coriander
½ teaspoon ground turmeric
¼–½ teaspoon chilli powder
1 teaspoon salt or to taste
300ml/½ pint/1⅓ cups warm water
½ teaspoon Garam Masala (pages 22–3)
1–2 green chillies, seeded and cut into juliennes

2 tablespoons chopped coriander (cilantro) leaves

1. Put the yogurt and besan (a little at a time) in a bowl and beat until smooth. Set aside.
2. Stir-fry the turnips until they are well browned. Drain on absorbent paper.
3. Reduce the heat slightly, add the shahi jeera, cloves and onion. Fry until lightly browned, about 8–9 minutes.
4. Reduce the heat to low and add the ginger. Stir-fry for 30 seconds.
5. Add the coriander, turmeric and chilli powder and stir-fry for 30 seconds. Make sure the pan is not too hot; if it is, remove from the heat and cool for a minute or so. Add half the yogurt mixture and bring to a very slow simmer. Now add the remaining yogurt and let it bubble very gently until the ghee rises to the top.
6. Add the fried turnips, salt and water. Stir and mix well. Cover and simmer very gently for 25–30 minutes or until the turnips are tender.
7. Add the garam masala, chillies and coriander (cilantro) leaves. Stir, remove from heat and serve.

Preparation time: 15 minutes
Cooking time: 30–35 minutes
Serving ideas: Serve with Family Naan (pages 152–4) and a chutney.
Variation: Substitute half the turnips with potatoes.
Use suran (yam) instead of turnips.
Suitable for freezing.

Dum-Aloo Dalchini

(New Potatoes with Cinnamon)

Serves 4

Packed with wonderful aromatic spices, this is a lovely way to serve new potatoes. I have used ghee for a richer flavour, but you can use oil if you wish. Butter is not suitable because of the fairly high temperature needed to fry the potatoes. You can, however, use a mixture of oil and butter.

450g/1lb/3 cups small new potatoes
50g/2oz/¼ cup ghee (see page 21)
1 teaspoon fennel seeds
4 x 2.5cm/1 inch pieces cassia bark or cinnamon sticks
6 whole cloves
2 bay leaves, crumbled
1 large onion (about 225g/8oz/2 cups), finely chopped
4cm/1½ inch cube root ginger, peeled and finely grated
½ teaspoon ground turmeric
2 teaspoons ground cumin
¼–½ teaspoon chilli powder
100g/4oz/½ cup canned chopped tomatoes including juice
1 teaspoon salt or to taste
600ml/1 pint/2½ cups warm water

½ teaspoon dried mint or 1 tablespoon finely chopped fresh mint
75ml/3 fl oz/⅓ cup single cream
½ teaspoon Garam Masala (pages 22–3)
2 tablespoons chopped coriander (cilantro) leaves

1. Scrub or scrape the potatoes, wash and dry thoroughly. Using a sharp knife, make several deep incisions in each potato without cutting right through. This will enable the flavours to penetrate the potatoes.
2. Heat the ghee in a sauté pan over a medium/high heat. When hot, fry the potatoes until well browned. Keep moving them around the pan to ensure even browning, they will brown very quickly towards the end. Turn off the heat and remove the potatoes with a slotted spoon and drain on absorbent paper. Let the fat cool for a minute or so then turn on the heat to low.
3. Add the fennel, cassia or cinnamon, cloves and bay leaves, and stir-fry for 15 seconds. Do not worry if you have browned potato crust in the pan, this will add plenty of flavour to the dish.
4. Increase the heat to medium and add the onion and ginger. Stir-fry for 4–5 minutes or until the onion is soft.
5. Add the turmeric, cumin and chilli powder. Stir-fry for 30 seconds and add the tomatoes. Stir-fry for 2–3 minutes or until the fat rises to the top.
6. Add the fried potatoes, salt and water. Bring to the boil and cook for 2 minutes. Stir once to re-position the potatoes, then reduce the heat to low. Cover the pan and simmer for 20 minutes. Stir occasionally and re-position potatoes.

7. Add the mint and cream and increase the heat to medium. Cook for 5 minutes. Stir in the garam masala and coriander (cilantro) leaves, remove from the heat and serve.

Preparation time: 25 minutes
Cooking time: 30–35 minutes
Serving ideas: Serve with Peshawari Naan (pages 155–7) and Tarka Dhal (pages 111–12) or Dhal Panchrattan (pages 107–8) makes an excellent optional extra side dish if you are entertaining.
Not suitable for freezing.

Aloo Ki Bhaji [V]

(Spiced Potatoes)

Serves 4

The word 'bhaji' is often confused with 'bhajiya' in this country. This is due to the way 'onion bhaji', a deep fried snack, is spelt on some restaurant menus. Bhaji is a traditional vegetable dish with little or no sauce.

4 tablespoons sunflower or corn oil
½ teaspoon black mustard seeds
1 teaspoon cumin seeds
8–10 curry leaves (optional)
1 onion (about 175g/6oz/1½ cups), finely sliced
1–2 green chillies, seeded and finely chopped
1 tablespoon dhanna-jeera powder
1 teaspoon ground turmeric
¼–½ teaspoon chilli powder (optional)
2 small ripe tomatoes, skinned and chopped
1 teaspoon salt or to taste
450g/1lb/3 cups old potatoes, boiled, peeled and cut into
  2.5cm/ 1 inch cubes
300ml/½ pint/1⅓ cups warm water
2 tablespoons finely chopped coriander (cilantro) leaves

1. Heat the oil in a medium saucepan over a low heat. When hot add the mustard seeds. As soon as they pop, add the cumin and curry leaves (if used). Increase the heat to medium and add the onion and chillies, and stir-fry for 6–7 minutes or until the onion begins to colour.
2. Add the dhanna-jeera powder, turmeric and chilli powder (if used). Stir-fry for 30 seconds, add the tomatoes and stir-fry for 1 minute.
3. Add the salt, potatoes and water, stir and cook for 4–5 minutes.
4. Stir in the coriander (cilantro) leaves, remove from the heat and serve.

Preparation time: 20–25 minutes, plus time to boil potatoes
Cooking time: 10–12 minutes
Serving ideas: Serve with Family Naan (pages 152–4) or Methi ki Roti (pages 158–9) or any other bread, even garlic bread!
Not suitable for freezing.

Kaddu Malai

(Creamed Butternut Squash)

Serves 4–6

One of my lovely childhood memories came flooding back when I was testing this recipe. My mother cooked this dish to perfection, using pumpkin, in a blackened heavy cast iron karahi. The rich golden colour of the pumpkin showed off beautifully in the black karahi and it made a pretty picture with fresh coriander (cilantro) leaves on top.

1 butternut squash or a small pumpkin (about 550g/1¼lb/4 cups)
2 potatoes (about 200g/7oz/1⅓ cups)
3 tablespoons sunflower or vegetable oil
2 x 2.5cm/1 inch pieces cassia bark or cinnamon sticks
4 green cardamom pods, split to the top of each pod
4 whole cloves
8 cloves garlic, peeled and crushed
1 small onion (about 100g/4oz/1 cup), finely chopped
1 tablespoon ground cumin
1 teaspoon ground turmeric
½–1 teaspoon crushed dried red chillies
100g/4oz/½ cup canned chopped tomatoes including juice

2.5cm/1 inch cube root ginger, peeled and grated
1 teaspoon salt or to taste
350ml/12 fl oz/1½ warm water
½ teaspoon Garam Masala (pages 22–3)
75ml/3 fl oz/⅓ single cream
2 tablespoon finely chopped coriander (cilantro) leaves

1. Halve or quarter the butternut squash or pumpkin and remove the seeds. Peel and cut into 2.5cm/1 inch cubes.
2. Peel the potatoes and cut into 1cm/½ inch cubes.
3. Preheat a karahi or wok over low heat for 1–2 minutes, then add the oil. When hot, add the cassia or cinnamon, cardamom and cloves. Let the spices sizzle for 30 seconds.
4. Add the garlic, stir-fry for 30 seconds, then add the onion. Increase to a medium heat and stir-fry for 6–7 minutes or until the onion begins to colour.
5. Add the cumin, turmeric and crushed chillies, stir-fry for 30 seconds and add the tomatoes. Stir-fry for 4–5 minutes or until the oil separates from the spice paste and begins to float.
6. Add the ginger, stir-fry for 1 minute then add the pumpkin, potatoes, salt and water. Increase the heat to high, bring to the boil and cook for 2–3 minutes. Now reduce the heat to low and cover the pan with a lid or a piece of foil. Cook for 20–25 minutes, stirring occasionally.
7. Add the garam masala, cream and half the coriander (cilantro) leaves. Stir and cook for 1 minute, then remove from the heat. Serve garnished with the remaining coriander (cilantro) leaves.

Preparation time: 20–25 minutes

Cooking time: 35 minutes

Serving ideas: Serve with Family Naan (pages 152–4) or Kashmiri Roti (pages 150–1).

Suitable for freezing, though the texture of cooked potatoes will change slightly.

Brinjal Bhaji V

(Spiced Aubergine (Eggplant))

Serves 4–6

Aubergine (eggplant) is normally soaked to remove the bitterness from the skin. Aubergines (eggplants) have now been developed with little bitterness, so to reduce preparation time, you can cook them without soaking, as long as they are tender and very fresh.

- 2 large aubergines (eggplants) (about 550g/1¼lb/4 cups total)
- 1 large onion (about 250g/8oz/2 cups), roughly chopped
- 2.5cm/1 inch cube root ginger, peeled and roughly chopped
- 6 cloves garlic, peeled and roughly chopped
- 1–2 long slim dried red chillies, roughly chopped
- 3–4 tablespoons water
- 4 tablespoons sunflower or corn oil
- ½ teaspoon black mustard seeds
- ½ teaspoon cumin seeds
- ½ teaspoon ground fennel
- 1 teaspoon ground coriander
- ½ teaspoon ground cumin
- 1 teaspoon ground turmeric
- 150g/5oz/1⅔ cups canned chopped tomatoes including juice

1 teaspoon salt or to taste
1 tablespoon tomato purée (paste)
450ml/¾ pint/2 cups warm water
½ teaspoon Garam Masala (pages 22–3)
2 tablespoons finely chopped coriander (cilantro) leaves

1. Quarter the aubergines (eggplants) lengthwise, then cut each quarter lengthwise into half. Cut into 2.5cm/1 inch chunks and soak in salted water for 30 minutes if you wish. Drain and rinse well.
2. Purée the onions, ginger, garlic and red chillies with the 3–4 tablespoons water in a food processor or liquidizer.
3. Heat the oil in a medium saucepan over a moderate heat. When hot but not smoking, add the mustard seeds. As soon as they pop, add the cumin seeds and stir-fry for 15 seconds.
4. Add the puréed ingredients and cook for 3–4 minutes. Reduce the heat to low and cook for a further 2 minutes.
5. Add the ground fennel, coriander, cumin and turmeric. Continue to cook for 2–3 minutes and add half the tomatoes. Increase the heat slightly and cook for 2–3 minutes. Add the remaining tomatoes and cook for a further 2–3 minutes or until the oil floats on top of the spice paste.
6. Add the salt, tomato purée, warm water and aubergine (eggplant), stir once, and bring to the boil. Reduce the heat to medium and cook for 10 minutes, uncovered. Stir well several times to ensure even cooking. The aubergine will float on the liquid during this time. When it begins to soak up the liquid, it will sink. When this happens, reduce the heat to low and simmer for 5 minutes, stirring well 2–3 times.

7. Sprinkle with the garam masala and coriander (cilantro) leaves. Stir again, remove from the heat and serve.

Preparation time: 15 minutes, plus soaking aubergine (eggplant)
Cooking time: 30 minutes
Serving ideas: Serve with Family Naan (pages 152–4) accompanied by a protein-rich dish such as Dhal Makhani (pages 113–14) or Dhal Panchrattan (pages 107–8).
Not suitable for freezing.

Do-Piaza Khumb V

(Mushroom Do-Piaza)

Serves 4

Do-Piaza is a Mogul term and it means any meat cooked with vegetables with lashings of onions. However, I have created this vegetarian version with mushrooms as the main ingredient.

1 small onion (about 100g/4oz/1 cup), roughly chopped
1cm/½ inch cube root ginger, peeled and roughly chopped
4 cloves garlic, peeled and chopped
1 green chilli, seeded and chopped
3–4 tablespoons water
4 tablespoons sunflower or corn oil
1 small onion (about 100g/4oz/1 cup), very finely chopped
2 teaspoons ground coriander
1½ teaspoons ground cumin
¼ teaspoon crushed dried chillies
1 teaspoon ground turmeric
10g/4oz/½ cup canned chopped tomatoes including juice
1 tablespoon tomato purée (paste)
1 teaspoon salt or to taste
375g/13oz/4⅓ cups closed cup mushrooms, thickly sliced
90g/3½oz/⅔ cup frozen garden peas or cooked fresh peas

75ml/3 fl oz/⅓ cup warm water
½ teaspoon Garam Masala (pages 22–3)

1. Purée the onion, ginger, garlic and fresh chilli with the 3–4 tablespoons of water in a food processor or liquidizer.
2. Preheat the oil in a medium saucepan over a moderate heat. When hot but not smoking, add the chopped onion and stir-fry for 3–4 minutes or until beginning to colour.
3. Add the ground coriander, cumin and crushed chillies. Stir-fry for 30 seconds, then add the puréed ingredients and stir-fry over a low heat for 3–4 minutes.
4. Add the turmeric and half the tomatoes, increase the heat to medium, and cook for 2–3 minutes. Add the remaining tomatoes and cook for 2–3 minutes or until the oil separates out.
5. Add the tomato purée (paste), salt, mushrooms, peas and warm water, stir and mix well. Reduce the heat to low and simmer, uncovered, for 5–6 minutes. By this time, the natural juices from the mushrooms, combined with the little cooking liquid will produce a thick, paste-like sauce.
6. Sprinkle with the garam masala and cook for 1 minute. Remove from the heat and serve.

Preparation time: 20–25 minutes
Cooking time: 20 minutes
Serving ideas: Serve with Family Naan (pages 152–4) or Peshawari Naan (pages 155–7), Channa Dhal Masala (pages 104–6) makes an excellent accompaniment.
Suitable for freezing.
Variation: Use cooked sliced green beans instead of peas.

Peshawari Paneer

(Peshawar-style Spiced Cheese)

Serves 4

Although Balti cooking is losing momentum in the rest of Britain, it is still a hot favourite in Birmingham. Here's a quick Balti recipe for you to try at home.

50g/2oz/¼ cup ghee or unsalted butter (page 21)
200g/7oz/1 cup paneer, cut into 2.5cm/1 inch cubes
2 x 2.5cm/1 inch pieces cassia bark or cinnamon sticks
4 cardamom pods, split to the top of each pod
8 cloves garlic, peeled and pounded to a pulp
1 onion (about 175g/6oz/1½ cups), finely chopped
1 green chilli, seeded and cut into juliennes
1 tablespoon dhanna-jeera powder
½ teaspoon ground turmeric
¼–½ teaspoon chilli powder
150g/5oz/⅔ cup canned chopped tomatoes including juice
1 tablespoon mint leaves, finely chopped or ½ teaspoon dried mint
75g/3oz/½ cup frozen garden peas, thawed, or cooked fresh peas
185g/6oz/1 cup frozen sweetcorn, thawed, or canned sweet corn, drained and rinsed
40g/1½oz/⅓ cup raw cashews, split

25g/1oz/⅕ cup seedless raisins
1 teaspoon salt or to taste
350ml/12 fl oz/1½ cups warm water
½ teaspoon Garam Masala (pages 22–3)

1. Preheat a karahi or wok over medium heat for 1–2 minutes, then add the ghee or butter. When hot, turn the heat down to low and fry the cubes of paneer, in batches if necessary, until lightly browned. Drain on absorbent paper.
2. In the same fat, fry the cassia and cardamom for 15 seconds. Add the garlic and stir-fry for 30 seconds or until lightly browned.
3. Add the onions and chilli and increase the heat to medium. Stir-fry for 4 minutes or until the onions are soft and just beginning to colour.
4. Add the dhanna-jeera powder, turmeric and chilli powder. Stir-fry for 1 minute and add tomatoes and mint. Stir-fry for 1 minute.
5. Add the peas, sweetcorn, cashews, raisins and salt. Stir-fry for 2 minutes, then add the water and cook for 2 minutes.
6. Add the paneer, cover the pan with a lid or a piece of foil and reduce the heat to low. Cook for 5 minutes.
7. Sprinkle with the garam masala, stir, remove from heat and serve.

Preparation time: 20–25 minutes

Cooking time: 18–20 minutes

Serving ideas: Serve with Family Naan (pages 152–4) or Soda Naan (pages 160–2).

Variation: Use tofu or Cyprus halloumi cheese instead of paneer.

Khumb-Aloo V

(Mushrooms with Potatoes)

Serves 4–6

Mushrooms and potatoes make a wonderful combination. This is a quick recipe using pre-boiled potatoes, which you can store in the fridge for a couple of days once they are boiled.

350g/12oz/4 cups large open cap mushrooms
1 onion (about 175g/6oz/1½ cups), roughly chopped
5–6 cloves garlic, peeled and roughly chopped
2.5cm/1 inch cube root ginger, peeled and roughly chopped
3 tablespoons sunflower or corn oil
2 tablespoons tomato purée (paste)
200g/7oz/1 cup canned chopped tomatoes including juice
1½ teaspoons ground cumin
2 teaspoons ground coriander
½–1 teaspoon chilli powder
1 teaspoon ground turmeric
1 teaspoon salt or to taste
275ml/8 fl oz/1 cup warm water
225g/8oz/⅔ cup old potatoes, boiled, peeled and cut into
  2.5cm/1 inch cubes
¼ teaspoon Garam Masala (pages 22–3)
2 tablespoons finely chopped coriander (cilantro) leaves

1. Quarter the mushrooms and cut each quarter into two.
2. Purée the onion, garlic and ginger with the 3–4 tablespoons of water in a blender or food processor.
3. Preheat the oil in a medium pan over medium heat for 1–2 minutes. When hot add the puréed ingredients and cook for 4–5 minutes.
4. Add the tomato purée (paste) and cook for 1 minute, then add half the tomatoes. Increase the heat slightly and cook for 1 minute.
5. Add the ground cumin, coriander, chilli powder and turmeric. Stir-fry for 1 minute, then add the remaining tomatoes. Reduce the heat to low and continue to cook for 2–3 minutes, stirring frequently.
6. Add the mushrooms, salt and water, cook for 2 minutes. Cover the pan and simmer for 5 minutes.
7. Add the potatoes, cover again and simmer for 3–4 minutes.
8. Sprinkle with the garam masala and fresh coriander (cilantro). Stir, cook for 1 minute, remove from the heat and serve.

Preparation time: 15–20 minutes, plus boiling potatoes
Cooking time: 18–20 minutes
Serving ideas: Serve with Family Naan (pages 152–4) and Rajma Masala (pages 109–10) or other protein-rich dish.
Suitable for freezing before adding the potatoes.
What to do with leftovers: Besides reheating to use as before, you can mix it with Sada Chawal (pages 142–3) to make a delicious instant mushroom pulao. Garnish with fresh coriander and serve with Dhal Makhani (pages 113–14) and a raita. There is no hard and fast rule about the proportion of cooked vegetables to rice.

You can use as much or as little as you like to freshly cooked Basmati rice.

Sabzi Besan Ki V

(Vegetables with Gram Flour)

Serves 4–6

'Besan', a special flour made of dried gram or chickpeas (garbanzo beans), is available in Asian stores, health food shops and some good supermarkets. It can be stored like ordinary flour, in a cool dry place.

4 leeks (about 450g/1lb/4 cups)
1 red pepper (about 200g/7oz/1¾ cups)
4 tablespoons sunflower or corn oil
½ teaspoon black mustard seeds
½ teaspoon cumin seeds
10–12 fenugreek seeds
8 cloves garlic, peeled and crushed
¼ teaspoon crushed dried red chillies
1 teaspoon salt or to taste
2 tablespoons chopped coriander (cilantro) leaves
125g/4oz/¾ cup besan (gram flour), sifted

1. Trim the leeks and halve them lengthwise. Wash thoroughly making sure you remove any grit between the leaves. Holding 3–4 halves of leeks together, slice them finely.

2. Remove the seeds and pith from the pepper and cut into 2.5cm/1 inch strips.
3. Preheat the oil in a non-stick sauté pan over medium heat for 1–2 minutes. Reduce the heat. When hot but not smoking, reduce the heat slightly and add the mustard seeds. As soon as they pop, add the cumin and fenugreek and follow with the garlic. Stir-fry for 1 minute.
4. Add the crushed chillies, stir-fry for 30 seconds and add the leeks, pepper slices and salt. Increase the heat to medium and stir-fry for 5 minutes.
5. Add the coriander (cilantro) leaves and 2 tablespoons of water, then sprinkle the besan evenly over the vegetables. Stir-fry for 1½ minutes and remove from the heat.

Preparation time: 20 minutes
Cooking time: 10 minutes
Serving ideas: Serve with Kashmir ki Roti (pages 150–1) or Sada Chawal (pages 142–3) and Aloo Choley (pages 132–3).
Not suitable for freezing.
What to do with leftovers: Use as a filling for spicy toasted sandwiches (excellent made in an electric toasted sandwich maker).
Variation: Add equal quantities of onion and cabbage instead of leeks. Stir-fry the onions for 2–3 minutes before adding the cabbage and pepper slices.

Shakahari Rogan Josh

(Vegetarian Rogan Josh)

Serves 4–6

Rogan Josh, a famous Kashmiri dish, is equally popular in India and abroad. I have created this vegetarian version using quorn which is nutritious, tasty and very versatile. Quorn is widely available in supermarkets and is very compatible with spices.

2 tablespoons sunflower or soya oil
25g/1oz ghee or unsalted butter (page 21)
4–5 cloves garlic, peeled and crushed to a pulp
4cm/1½ inch cube of root ginger, peeled and finely grated
1 large onion (225g/8oz/2 cups), finely chopped
½ teaspoon ground fennel
1½ teaspoons ground coriander
½ teaspoon ground turmeric
½ teaspoon chilli powder
1½ tablespoons tomato purée (paste)
350g/12oz/3 cups pack quorn pieces
225ml/8fl oz/1 cup warm water
1 teaspoon salt or to taste
½ teaspoon dried mint
125ml/4fl oz/½ cup single cream

½ teaspoon Garam Masala (page 22–3)
2 tablespoons chopped coriander (cilantro) leaves

1. Heat the oil and butter or ghee together in a pan over medium heat. Add the garlic, ginger and onion. Stir-fry for 7–8 minutes or until the onions are soft with a pale brown tinge.
2. Reduce the heat to low and add the fennel, coriander, turmeric and chilli powder. Stir-fry for 1 minute, then add 2 tablespoons of water and the tomato purée (paste). Cook for 2 minutes or until the oil surfaces the spices paste. Stir regularly.
3. Add the quorn and stir-fry over medium heat for 2 minutes, then add the water, salt and mint. Bring to the boil, cover the pan and simmer for 15 minutes.
4. Add the cream and garam masala and continue to simmer for 5 minutes, uncovered. Stir in the coriander (cilantro) leaves, remove from the heat and serve.

Preparation time: 15 minutes
Cooking time: 30 minutes
Serving ideas: Serve with Kesari Chawal (page 144–5) and a raita.

Makki-Khumb Jhal Frazi V

(Sweetcorn and Mushroom Jhal Frazi)

Serves 4–6

A quick and easy dish to prepare with an attractive and colourful appearance.

3 tablespoons cooking oil
1 large onion (about 225g/8oz/2 cups), finely sliced
2.5cm/1 inch cube root ginger, peeled and finely grated
1 green chilli, seeded and sliced
½ teaspoon chilli powder
½ teaspoon ground turmeric
1 teaspoon ground coriander
½ teaspoon ground cumin
275g/10oz/1¼ cups canned chopped tomatoes
225g/8oz/1 cup frozen sweetcorn, thawed, or canned sweetcorn, drained and rinsed
275g/10oz/3 cups closed cup mushrooms, sliced
1 tablespoon tomato purée (paste)
50ml/2 fl oz/¼ cup warm water
1 teaspoon salt or to taste
25g/1oz/¼ cup red pepper, diced
25g/1oz/¼ cup green pepper, diced

½ teaspoon Garam Masala (pages 22–3)
1 tablespoon chopped coriander (cilantro) leaves

1. In a sauté pan, heat the oil over a medium heat. Add the onion, ginger and chilli. Fry for 6–7 minutes or until soft and light golden brown.
2. Add the chilli powder, turmeric, coriander and cumin. Cook for 30 seconds.
3. Add half the tomatoes, increase the heat slightly and cook for 3–4 minutes or until the oil separates from the spice paste.
4. Add the sweetcorn, mushrooms, tomato purée (paste), and water. Cook for 3–4 minutes, then add the salt and red and green pepper. Cook for 1–2 minutes stirring continuously.
5. Add the remaining tomatoes, garam masala and coriander (cilantro) leaves. Cook for 1 minute, remove from the heat and serve.

Preparation time: 15 minutes
Cooking time: 20 minutes
Serving ideas: Serve with Family Naan (pages 152–4) accompanied by a protein-dish such as Channa Dhal Masala (pages 104–6).

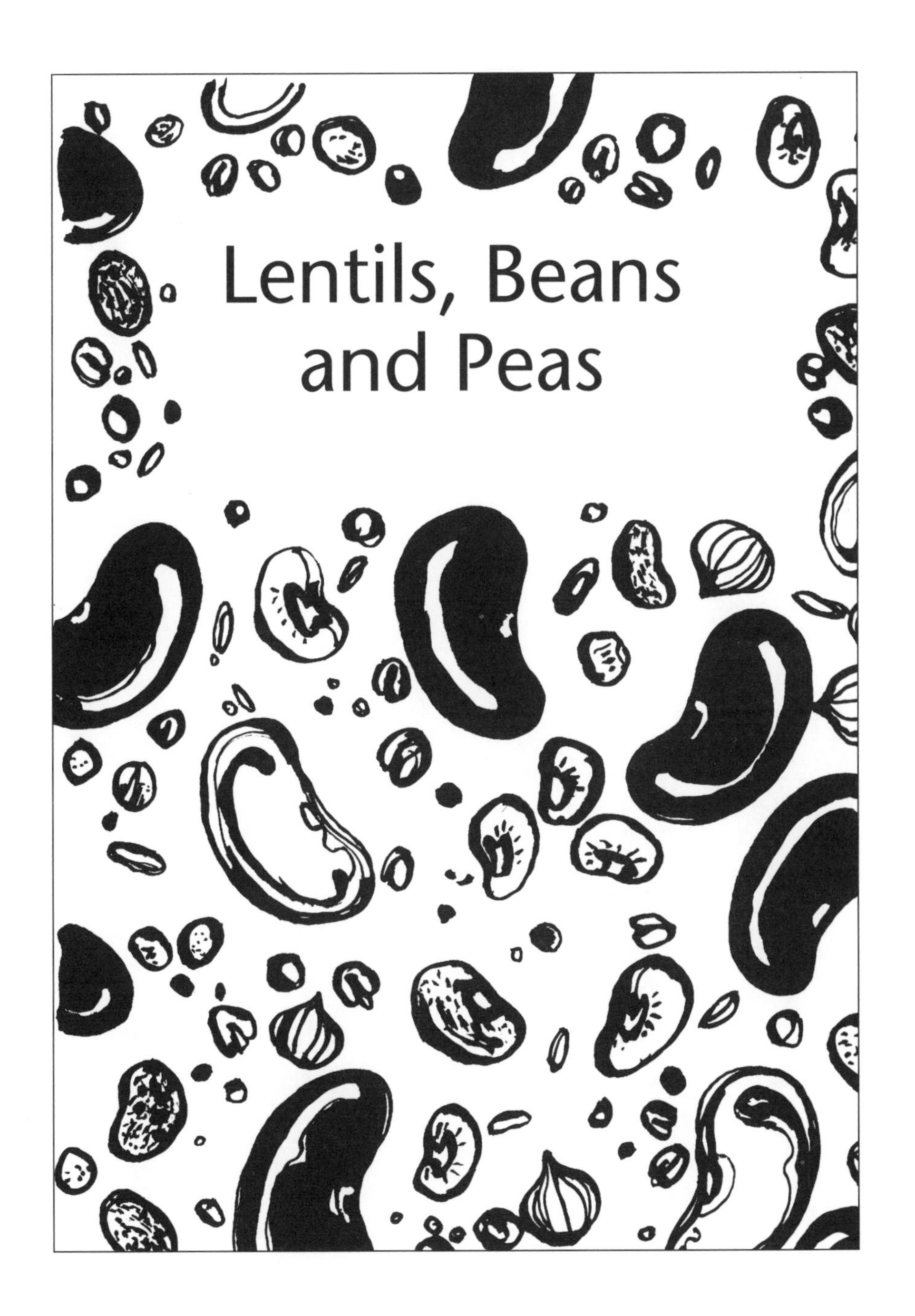
Lentils, Beans
and Peas

Lentils, beans and peas form a very important part of a vegetarian diet. Indian vegetarian food is a classic example of balanced, healthy and appetizing meals. It consists of high protein and high fibre with all the essential vitamins and nutrients.

The main source of protein is grains and pulses. These also have a high content of fibre, vitamins and minerals.

As you will see from the recipes in this chapter, lentils, beans and peas can be cooked in numerous ways to produce delicious and varied meals.

Sabut Mung Sabzi Ke Sath

(Mung Beans with Vegetables)

Serves 4

Mung beans are a wonderful source of vitamins and essential minerals. You can buy them from health food shops and Indian stores. You will have to remember to soak them overnight or in the morning (to cook in the same evening).

150g/5oz/¾ cup mung beans
300ml/½ pint/⅓ cup water
2 tablespoons sunflower or corn oil
½ teaspoon black mustard seeds
½ teaspoon cumin seeds
3–4 cloves garlic, peeled and crushed
2.5cm/1 inch cube root ginger, peeled and grated
50g/2oz/½ cup red pepper, cut into 2.5cm/1 inch dice
1 small onion (about 100g/4oz/1 cup), coarsely chopped
100g/4oz/¾ cup carrots, halved lengthwise and thinly sliced
100g/4oz/1 cup cauliflower, divided into 5mm/¼ inch florets
1 teaspoon salt or to taste
½ teaspoon chilli powder
100g/4oz/½ cup canned chopped tomatoes including juice
2 tablespoons chopped coriander (cilantro) leaves

1. Pick over the mung beans, wash and soak in plenty of cold water overnight. Drain and rinse several times.
2. Put the beans and water in a saucepan and place over a high heat. Bring to the boil, partially cover the pan and cook over medium heat for 5–6 minutes or until it stops being frothy. Reduce the heat to low, cover and simmer for 15 minutes or until the beans are tender and the liquid reduces to about 2–3 tablespoons.
3. Heat the oil in a sauté pan over medium heat. When hot but not smoking, add the mustard seeds followed by the cumin. As soon as the seeds pop, add the garlic, ginger, red pepper and onion. Stir-fry for 1 minute.
4. Add the carrots and cauliflower, stir-fry for a further minute, then add the salt and chilli powder. Stir-fry for 1–2 minutes.
5. Add the cooked beans, along with the cooking liquid left in the pan. Stir-fry for 2–3 minutes or until the beans and vegetables are well blended.
6. Add the tomatoes and stir-fry for 1–2 minutes. Stir in coriander leaves, remove from the heat and serve.

Preparation time: 25 minutes, plus time for soaking beans
Cooking time: 25 minutes
Serving ideas: Serve with Methi ki Roti (pages 158–9) accompanied by Do-piaza Khumb (pages 85–6).
Suitable for freezing.

Channa Dhal Masala V

(Spiced Bengal Gram Dhal)

Serves 4

A superb lentil delicacy with the distinctive flavours of fennel and dried fenugreek leaves (Kasoori methi). If you cannot get channa dhal, use yellow split peas instead, though the latter does not have the same flavour.

175g/6oz/¾ cup channa dhal or yellow split peas
600ml/1 pint/2½ cups water
3 tablespoons sunflower or corn oil
2 x 2.5cm/1 inch cinnamon sticks
1 teaspoon fennel seeds
6–8 cloves garlic, peeled and crushed
½ teaspoon crushed dried chillies
1 onion (about 175g/6oz/1½ cups), finely sliced
1–2 green chillies, seeded and cut into juliennes
1 teaspoon salt or to taste
1 teaspoon ground fennel
1 teaspoon ground cumin
225g/8oz/1 cup canned chopped tomatoes including juice
1 tablespoon Kasoori methi, dried stalks removed

1 teaspoon Garam Masala (pages 22–3)
2 tablespoons chopped coriander (cilantro) leaves

1. Pick over the dhal and wash in several changes of water. Soak in plenty of cold water for 2 hours. Longer would not matter. Drain thoroughly.
2. Put the lentils and water in a saucepan, add to water and place over a high heat. Bring to the boil, and boil steadily for 8–10 minutes. Reduce the heat to low, cover and simmer for 30–35 minutes until the dhal is tender and has absorbed nearly all the water. The dhal at this stage should be rather like the consistency of baked beans. Remove from the heat and set aside. (At this stage, you can cool and refrigerate the dhal for up to 48 hours.)
3. In a medium sized pan, heat the oil over low heat for 1–2 minutes. Add the cinnamon and fennel seeds, and let them sizzle for 15–20 seconds, then add the garlic and stir-fry for 1 minute.
4. Add the crushed chillies and increase the heat to medium. Add the onion and fresh chillies, stir-fry for 2 minutes, add the salt, and cook for a further 3–4 minutes, stirring frequently.
5. Add the ground fennel, cumin and half the tomatoes. Stir-fry for 2–3 minutes or until you can see oil floating on the surface.
6. Add the cooked dhal, increase the heat slightly and stir-fry for 4–5 minutes. Add the remaining tomatoes, Kasoori methi, garam masala and remaining tomatoes. Stir-fry for 1 minute. Stir in the coriander (cilantro) leaves, remove from the heat and serve.

Preparation time: 30 minutes (includes pre-cooking the lentils), plus soaking time for dhal

Cooking time: 15 minutes

Serving ideas: Serve with Family Naan (pages 152–4) or Soda Naan (pages 160–2), accompanied by Gobi Andey (pages 56–7) or Saag-Aloo (pages 130–1).

Suitable for freezing.

Dhal Panchrattan

(Five Types of Lentils)

Serves 4

This is a delicacy from the state of Punjab, using five types of lentils – 'panch' meaning five' and 'rattan' meaning 'jewels'. You can try other combinations too. Replace the whole moong dhal with urid dhal and channa dhal with tuvar dhal.

40g/1½oz/⅕ cup masoor dhal (red split lentils)
40g/1½oz/⅕ cup moong dhal (yellow split lentils)
40g/1½oz/⅕ cup channa dhal or yellow split peas
40g/1½oz/⅕ cup whole masoor dhal (whole brown lentils)
40g/1½oz/⅕ cup whole moong dhal (mung beans)
900ml/1½ pints/3¾ cups water
2 teaspoons ground cumin
1 teaspoon ground turmeric
2 x 2.5cm/1 inch pieces cinnamon sticks
1 teaspoon salt or to taste
50g/2oz/¼ cup ghee or unsalted butter (page 21)
1 onion (about 175g/6oz/½ cup), finely chopped
1–2 green chillies, seeded and cut into juliennes
2.5cm/½ inch cube root ginger, peeled and cut into juliennes
¼ teaspoon crushed dried chillies

75g/3oz canned chopped tomatoes including juice
½ teaspoon Garam Masala (pages 22–3)
2 tablespoons chopped coriander (cilantro) leaves

1. Pick over each variety of lentils, mix together and wash in several changes of water. Soak them for 4–5 hours.
2. Put lentils and water in a saucepan over a high heat. Bring to the boil and cook for 10 minutes, skimming off scum as necessary.
3. Add the cumin, turmeric and cinnamon, stir and reduce the heat to low. Cover and simmer for 20–25 minutes, stirring occasionally. Stir in the salt and mash some of the lentils (about a quarter) with a spoon. Remove from the heat and set aside.
4. In a wok or a saucepan, melt the ghee or butter. Over a medium heat, fry the onions, fresh chillies and ginger for 3–4 minutes, then add the dried chillies. Stir-fry for a further 30 seconds and add the tomatoes. Stir-fry for 2 minutes, then stir in the garam masala and coriander (cilantro) leaves. Add this mixture to the cooked dhal, stir well and return the pan to the heat. Let the dhal bubble for 1 minute, remove from the heat and serve.

Preparation time: 20–25 minutes, plus time to soak lentils
Cooking time: 45–50 minutes
Serving ideas: Serve with Family Naan (pages 152–4) or Sada Chawal (pages 142–3).
Suitable for freezing.

Rajma Masala V

(Spiced Red Kidney Beans)

Serves 4

Red kidney beans are wonderful to cook with spices. The dried beans are normally soaked and boiled until tender before being cooked. If you use dried beans, boil the beans for 10–15 minutes, drain, rinse and then cook them in fresh water. This process is necessary to remove the toxins present in red kidney beans. For an easy alternative, I have used canned beans for this recipe.

1 onion (about 175g/6oz/1½ cups), roughly chopped
2.5cm/1 inch cube root ginger, peeled and roughly chopped
4 cloves garlic, peeled and roughly chopped
4 tablespoons sunflower or corn oil
2 teaspoons ground cumin
2 teaspoons ground coriander
½ teaspoon ground turmeric
¼–½ teaspoon chilli powder
1 tablespoon tomato purée (paste)
625g/1lb/2⅓ cups canned red kidney beans, drained
and rinsed
1 teaspoon salt or to taste
275ml/8 fl oz/1 cup warm water

3–4 green chillies (preferably the long slim ones)
½ teaspoon Garam Masala (pages 22–3)
2 tablespoons chopped coriander (cilantro) leaves

1. Purée the onion, ginger and garlic in a food processor.
2. In a saucepan or wok heat the oil over a medium heat. When hot, add the puréed ingredients and stir-fry for 4–5 minutes.
3. Reduce the heat to low, add the ground cumin and coriander, and stir-fry for 2 minutes. Add the turmeric, chilli powder and tomato purée (paste), and stir-fry for another minute or two.
4. Add the beans and salt, increase the heat to medium and stir-fry for 1 minute.
5. Add the water, and chillies, then simmer gently for 5 minutes, stirring frequently.
6. Sprinkle with garam masala, stir in the coriander (cilantro) leaves, remove from the heat and serve.

Preparation time: 10 minutes
Cooking time: 15 minutes
Serving ideas: Serve with Methi ki Roti (pages 158–9) or Khumb Pulao (pages 146–7).
Variation: Use black-eyed beans or butter beans.
Suitable for freezing.

Tarka Dhal

(Lentils with Spicy Hot Oil Seasoning)

Serves 4

Pulses have been an important and essential food item in India where the vast majority of the population is vegetarian. Evidence of pulses being eaten even in ancient times has been traced in the remains of Indus Valley Civilization, the world's third literate society.

1 teaspoon cumin seeds
½ teaspoon fennel seeds
175g/6oz/¾ cup masoor dhal (red split lentils)
750ml/1¼ pints/3¼ cups water
1 teaspoon ground turmeric
1 teaspoon salt or to taste
40g/1½oz ghee or unsalted butter (see page 21)
4 cloves garlic, peeled and roughly chopped then crushed
1–2 green chillies, seeded and cut into juliennes
2 small tomatoes, skinned and chopped (optional)
1 tablespoon chopped coriander (cilantro) leaves

1. Pick over and wash the dhal in several changes of water.
2. Put the dhal, water and turmeric into a saucepan over high heat, bring to the boil and cook for 3 minutes. Reduce the heat to low, partially cover the pan with a lid, and cook for 8–10 minutes or until it stops being frothy. Keep an eye on it, and add a little more water if necessary. Cover the pan fully and simmer for 25 minutes or until the lentils are tender and thick. At this stage, you can add more water if you find it too thick or dry. Stir in the salt and remove from heat.
3. In a small pan, melt the ghee or butter gently over a low heat. Add the fennel, cumin and garlic. Gently fry until the garlic is lightly browned.
4. Add the chillies and stir-fry for 30 seconds. Add the tomatoes (if used) and coriander (cilantro) leaves and stir-fry for 30 seconds. Pour this mixture over the cooked dhal, making sure you scrape off and add every bit of flavoured ghee and other ingredients in the pan. Stir and mix thoroughly with the dhal.

Preparation time: 10 minutes
Cooking time: 35–40 minutes
Serving ideas: Serve with Family Naan (pages 152–4) or Sada Chawal (pages 142–3) accompanied by Saag Aloo (pages 130–1) or Khumb-Aloo (pages 90–2).
Suitable for freezing.

Dhal Makhani

(Lentils with Butter)

Serves 4

This is probably the best known and best loved lentil delicacy in India, after Tarka Dhal. The lentils used here are whole brown lentils (whole masoor dhal). When skinned and split, they are known as red split lentils or masoor dhal. Whole masoor dhal is available in Asian stores and health food shops.

175g/6oz/¾ cup whole masoor dhal
1 tablespoon sunflower or corn oil
45 cloves garlic, peeled and puréed or crushed to a pulp
2.5cm/1 inch cube root ginger, peeled and finely grated
½ teaspoon ground turmeric
1 teaspoon ground cumin
½ teaspoon chilli powder
600ml/1 pint/2½ cups hot water
2 tomatoes (about 150g/5oz/¾ cup), skinned and chopped
2 tablespoons tomato purée (paste)
3–4 green chillies
1 teaspoon salt or to taste
½ teaspoon sugar
50g/2oz/¼ cup butter

200ml/7 fl oz/¾ cup single cream
2 tablespoons chopped coriander (cilantro) leaves

1. Pick over the lentils and wash in several changes of water. Soak for 3–4 hours or overnight if you wish. Drain well.
2. In a medium saucepan, heat the oil gently, then add the garlic, ginger, turmeric, ground cumin and chilli powder. Fry for 2 minutes and add the lentils and water. Bring to the boil over a high heat and cook for 1 minute. Reduce the heat to low, cover the pan with a lid, and simmer for 30–35 minutes, stirring half way through.
3. Mash about a quarter of the lentils with a wooden spoon. Add the tomatoes, tomato purée (paste), sugar, chillies, salt, butter and cream, and cook gently for 5 minutes, uncovered.
4. Add the coriander (cilantro) leaves, stir, remove from the heat and serve.

Preparation time: 15–20 minutes, plus soaking the lentils
Cooking time: 45 minutes
Serving ideas: Serve with Family Naan (pages 152–4) accompanied by Gobi-Aloo-Saag (pages 130–1) or Aloo ki Bhaji (pages 77–8).
Suitable for freezing.

Moong Dhal Jhal Frazi

(Stir-fried Yellow Split Lentils)

Serves 4

Moong dhal is derived from skinned and split whole moong dhal (mung beans) and is available from health food stores, good supermarkets and Asian grocers. Jhal frazi, or stir-frying, is a wonderful way to cook moong dhal as it is probably the fastest cooking lentil.

175g/6oz/¾ cup moong dhal
50g/2oz/¼ cup ghee (page 21)
3 x 2.5cm/1 inch pieces cinnamon sticks
4 green cardamom pods, split to the top of each pod
1cm/½ inch cube root ginger, peeled and cut into juliennes
1 large onion (about 225g/8oz/2 cups), finely sliced
1–2 long slim dried red chillies, chopped
1 teaspoon salt or to taste
5–6 cloves garlic, peeled and crushed
½ teaspoon ground turmeric
2 teaspoons ground cumin
450ml/¾pint/2 cups warm water
100g/4oz/½ cup canned chopped tomatoes including juice
4 green chillies
2 tablespoons chopped coriander (cilantro) leaves

1. Pick over the lentils and wash in several changes of water. Soak for 1–2 hours and drain.
2. In a wok or sauté pan, melt the ghee over medium heat. Add the cinnamon and cardamom pods, allow to sizzle for 15 seconds.
3. Add the ginger, stir-fry for 30 seconds, then add the onion, dried chillies and salt, and stir-fry for 4–5 minutes or until the onion begins to colour.
4. Add the garlic and turmeric and stir-fry for 30 seconds.
5. Add the moong dhal with the ground cumin. Stir-fry for 2–3 minutes, then add 150ml/¼ pint of the water. Increase the heat to high and stir-fry until the water dries up. Add the remaining water, bring to the boil and reduce the heat to medium. Cook for 12–15 minutes, stirring frequently.
6. Add the tomatoes and fresh chillies, stir-fry for 5 minutes, then add the coriander (cilantro). Stir-fry for 1 minute, remove from the heat and serve.

Preparation time: 10–15 minutes, plus soaking dhal
Cooking time: 30 minutes
Serving ideas: Serve with Peshawari Naan (pages 155–7) or Kaddu Malai (pages 79–81).

Adraki Moong Dhal [V]

(Mung Beans with Ginger)

Serves 4

Mung beans are an excellent source of vitamin C. They are easily available from health food stores, supermarkets and, of course, Asian grocers. This particular dish is good enough to eat on its own as a snack. The beans can be cooked in advance if you wish, and kept in the fridge for up to 36 hours. They can also be frozen: simply thaw and proceed from step 3. You can utilize any left over in many delicious ways as you will see from the ideas given below.

175g/6oz/¾ cup whole moong dhal (mung beans)
300ml/½pint/1⅓ cups water
2 tablespoons sunflower or corn oil
½ teaspoon black mustard seeds
½ teaspoon cumin seeds
1 teaspoon coriander seeds, pounded to a coarse texture
1 onion (about 175g/6oz/1½ cups), finely chopped
2.5cm/1 inch cube root ginger, peeled and cut into juliennes
1 green chilli, seeded and cut into juliennes
1 teaspoon salt or to taste
100g/4oz/½ cup canned chopped tomatoes including juice

¼ teaspoon crushed dried chillies
½ teaspoon Garam Masala (pages 22–3)

1. Pick over, wash and soak the mung beans overnight in plenty of cold water. Drain well.
2. Put the mung beans and water in a saucepan over a high heat. Bring to the boil, reduce the heat to medium, partially cover the pan and cook for 5–6 minutes. You will find that the beans will create quite a lot of froth when they are cooking. When the froth settles down, reduce the heat to low, cover and simmer for 15 minutes. The beans should be tender by this time and most of the water absorbed, leaving about 2 tablespoons. Remove the pan from the heat and set aside.
3. In a wok of sauté pan, heat the oil over medium heat. When hot but not smoking, add the mustard seeds. As soon as they pop, add the cumin and coriander. Stir-fry for 30 seconds and add the onion, ginger and fresh chilli. Stir-fry for 6–7 minutes or until the onion is soft and beginning to colour slightly.
4. Add the cooked beans, along with any cooking liquid left in the pan, and salt. Stir-fry for 3–4 minutes, then add the tomatoes and crushed chillies. Stir-fry for 2 minutes.
5. Sprinkle with the garam masala, stir-fry for 1 minute, remove from the heat and serve.

Preparation time: 15 minutes, plus soaking the beans
Cooking time: 30 minutes
Serving ideas: Serve with Methi ki Roti (pages 158–9) or Sada Chawal (pages 142–3) and Gobi Andey (pages 56–7).

What to do with leftovers: you can of course freeze any leftovers. Alternatively, dress up the leftovers to give a completely new look! Use it cold to make a lovely raita. Simply mix mung beans with enough thick set whole milk natural yogurt. You can also reheat and use it as a topping for jacket potatoes and serve with a mixed salad.

Variation: Use canned butter beans, well drained and rinsed.

Palak Choley V

(Spinach with Chickpeas)

Serves 4–6

The combination of spinach and chickpeas (garbanzo beans) is visually pleasing as well as being rich in all the vitamins and nutrients. I have used fresh spinach but you can use frozen if you wish. Do make sure it is frozen leaf spinach and not the purée.

1 large onion (about 225g/8oz/2 cups), roughly chopped
2.5cm/1 inch cube root ginger, peeled and roughly chopped
1 long slim dried red chilli, chopped
3 tablespoons sunflower or corn oil
1 teaspoon fennel seeds
6–8 cloves garlic, peeled and crushed
1 tablespoon dhanna-jeera powder
½ teaspoon ground turmeric
1 teaspoon paprika
1 tablespoon tomato purée (paste)
400g/14oz/2 cups can chickpeas (garbanzo beans), drained and rinsed
150ml/¼ pint/⅔ cup warm water
225g/8oz spinach, finely chopped
1 teaspoon salt or to taste

100g/4oz/½ cup canned chopped tomatoes including juice
½ teaspoon Garam Masala (pages 22–3)

1. Purée the onion, ginger and red chilli in a food processor until smooth.
2. Preheat a karahi, wok or sauté pan over medium heat for 1–2 minutes, then add the oil. When hot but not smoking, add the fennel seeds followed by the garlic. Stir-fry for 30 seconds.
3. Add the dhanna-jeera powder, stir-fry for 30 seconds, then add the puréed ingredients. Stir-fry for 3 minutes or until the oil surfaces the spice paste.
4. Add the turmeric, paprika and tomato purée (paste) and stir-fry for 1 minute.
5. Add the chickpeas (garbanzo beans) and water, bring to the boil then reduce the heat to low. Cover the karahi or wok with a lid or a piece of foil and simmer for 10 minutes.
6. Add the spinach and salt and increase the heat to medium-high. Stir-fry for 1 minute when the spinach will shrink and release its natural juices.
7. Add the tomatoes and stir-fry for 6–8 minutes, reducing the heat slightly if necessary. Sprinkle with the garam masala, stir-fry for 1 minute, then remove from the heat and serve.

Preparation time: 20–25 minutes
Cooking time: 25 minutes
Serving ideas: Serve with Soda Naan (pages 160–2) or Kashmir ki Roti (pages 150–1).
Suitable for freezing if fresh spinach is used.

Combination Recipes

In this chapter, I have created recipes for a few very quick dishes using a combination of lentils and vegetables. Using such a combination means you have a compeltely balanced and nourishing dish, often in one pot, without having to cook another complementary one.

A karahi, work or other similar heavy pan is ideal for these dishes.

Dhal-Saag-Gajjar V

(Lentils with Spinach and Carrot)

Serves 4–5

Here is a quick combination dish which is completely balanced. I like the idea of a 'combination dish' because you can also use two or more leftovers to create an entirely new taste!

100g/4oz/½ cup masoor dhal (red split lentils)
600ml/1 pint/2½ cups water
3 tablespoons sunflower or corn oil
3 cloves garlic, peeled and crushed
1cm/½ inch cube root ginger, peeled and grated
1 green chilli, seeded and chopped
1 small onion (about 100g/4oz/1 cup), finely chopped
1 tablespoon dhanna-jeera powder
¼–½ teaspoon chilli powder
½ teaspoon Garam Masala (pages 22–3)
½ teaspoon dried mint
225g/8oz/4 cups spinach, finely chopped or frozen leaf spinach, thawed and chopped
125ml/4fl oz sieved tomatoes or passata
100g/4oz/1 cup carrots, peeled, cut into batons and parboiled

1 teaspoon salt or to taste
2 tablespoons chopped coriander (cilantro) leaves

1. Pick over the lentils, wash in several changes of water and drain thoroughly.
2. Put the dhal and water in a saucepan over a high heat and bring to the boil. Reduce the heat to low and partially cover the pan. At this stage, the lentils will be quite frothy, cook until the froth disappears, then cover the pan fully. Do not cover while any froth is present, as this will cause the liquid to spill over. Simmer for 30 minutes or until the lentils are tender and thick. Remove the pan from the heat and set aside.
3. When hot but not smoking, stir-fry the garlic, ginger and fresh chilli for 30 seconds. Add the onion and stir-fry for 3–4 minutes. Reduce the heat and continue to fry for 3–4 minutes.
4. Add the dhanna-jeera powder, chilli powder, garam masala and mint, stir-fry for 1 minute, then add the spinach. Stir-fry for 2–3 minutes or until the spinach has wilted and released its natural juices.
5. Add the sieved tomatoes or passata and stir-fry for 2 minutes, then add the cooked dhal, carrots, potatoes and salt. Stir and mix thoroughly, bring to boiling point, then reduce the heat to low and simmer for 2–3 minutes. Stir in the coriander leaves, remove from the heat and serve.

Preparation time: 30 minutes
Cooking time: 30 minutes including pre-cooking lentils
Serving ideas: Serve with Peshawari Naan (pages 87–9) and/or Sada Chawal (pages 142–3).

Khumb-Aloo-Mattar V

(Mushrooms, Potatoes and Peas)

Serves 4–6

Use whole button mushrooms and new potatoes for this recipe. Throw in a few peas for a contrast in colour and you have a dazzling and delicious dish in a jiffy!

4 tablespoons sunflower or corn oil
1 small onion (about 100g/4oz/1 cup), finely chopped
3 cloves garlic, peeled and crushed
2 teaspoons ground coriander
1 teaspoon ground cumin
¼–½ teaspoon chilli powder
1 tablespoon tomato purée (paste)
175ml/6 fl oz/⅔ cup canned sieved tomatoes or passata
225g/8oz/2 cups button mushrooms
75g/3oz/½ cup frozen garden peas
300g/11oz/2 cups small new potatoes, scrubbed, boiled and halved
300ml/½ pint/1⅓ cups warm water
1 teaspoon salt or to taste
½ teaspoon dried mint

¼ teaspoon Garam Masala (pages 22–3)
2 tablespoons chopped coriander (cilantro) leaves

1. In a karahi, wok or other heavy pan, heat the oil over medium heat. When hot, stir-fry the onion for 3–4 minutes, add the garlic, ground coriander, cumin and chilli powder. Reduce the heat slightly and stir-fry for 1 minute.
2. Add the tomato purée (paste) and base sauce, and stir-fry for 2–3 minutes, reducing the heat to low as it begins to dry up and oil starts floating on the surface.
3. Add the sieved tomatoes or passata and simmer for 1–2 minutes. Add the mushrooms, peas and potatoes, stir-fry for 2 minutes and add the water, salt and mint. Bring to the boil, cover with a lid or a piece of foil, and reduce the heat to low. Simmer for 8–10 minutes.
4. Stir in the garam masala and coriander (cilantro) leaves, remove from the heat and serve.

Preparation time: 15 minutes
Cooking time: 20 minutes
Serving ideas: Serve with Family Naan (pages 152–4) or Soda Naan (pages 160–2) accompanied by Dhal Makhani (pages 113–14), if wished.

Gobi-Aloo-Saag

(Cauliflower, Potatoes and Spinach)

Serves 4–6

This is a good combination with easily available vegetables. It only takes a few minutes to cook, especially if you have potatoes already boiled. I find it very useful to tuck away a few boiled potatoes in the fridge. You can find all sorts of ways to rustle up something delicious (for instance, cubed and fried quickly to make a raita with a dash of cumin) for a midweek meal.

3 tablespoons sunflower or soya oil
½ teaspoon black mustard seeds
1–2 dried red chillies, chopped
3–4 cloves garlic, crushed
1 medium onion, finely sliced
½ teaspoon ground turmeric
1 teaspoon ground coriander
¼–½ teaspoon chilli powder
350g/12oz/3 cups cauliflower florets (1cm/½ inch diameter)
225g/8oz/4 cups spinach, fresh or frozen, chopped
1 teaspoon salt to taste
225g/8oz/1 cup fresh tomatoes, skinned and chopped or canned tomatoes, drained

150ml/5fl oz/⅔ cup single cream
350g/12oz/2¼ cups boiled potatoes, peeled and cut into
2.5cm/1 inch cubes
½ teaspoon Garam Masala

1. In a medium sized saucepan, heat the oil over low-medium heat. When hot, add the mustard seeds. As soon as they pop, add the chillies and garlic. Stir-fry for 30 seconds and add the onion. Increase the heat slightly and fry the onion for 6–7 minutes or until soft and pale golden brown.
2. Add the turmeric, coriander and chilli powder. Fry for 1 minute.
3. Add the cauliflower, spinach and salt. Stir well, reduce the heat to low and cover the pan. Cook for 10–12 minutes.
4. Add the tomatoes, cream, potatoes and Garam Masala. Stir well and cook, uncovered, for 6–7 minutes or until the cauliflower is tender, but still firm and the sauce has coated the vegetables.

Preparation time: 20 minutes
Cooking time: 20–25 minutes
Serving ideas: Serve with any bread or rice accompanied by a chutney, if liked.

Aloo-Choley

(Potatoes with Chickpeas (Garbanzo Beans))

Serves 4–6

A well-known delicacy from the state of Punjab in Northern India, Aloo-Choley is very popular all over India. You can use dried chickpeas (garbanzo beans) which you will need to soak overnight and cook before adding to the spices. Alternatively, use canned chickpeas which are ready to use and work extremely well.

3 tablespoons sunflower or corn oil
2 x 2.5cm/1 inch cinnamon sticks
2.5cm/1 inch cube root ginger, peeled and cut into juliennes
1–2 green chillies, seeded and cut into juliennes
6 cloves garlic, peeled and pounded to a pulp
1 onion (about 175g/6oz/1½ cups), finely sliced
1 teaspoon salt or to taste
1 teaspoon ground cumin
½ teaspoon ground turmeric
¼–½ teaspoon chilli powder
100g/4oz/½ cup passata or canned tomatoes with juice, sieved
150ml/¼ pint/⅔ cup warm water
175g/6oz/1¼ cups potatoes, peeled and cut into 2.5cm/
1 inch cubes

400g/14oz/2 cups can chickpeas (garbanzos), drained and well rinsed
2 teaspoons Kasoori methi, dried stalks removed
¼ teaspoon Garam Masala (page 22–3)
2 tablespoons chopped coriander (cilantro) leaves

1. In a heavy based saucepan, heat the oil gently over low heat. Add the cinnamon, ginger, fresh chillies and garlic. Fry gently for 1 minute.
2. Add the onion and salt and increase the heat slightly. Stir-fry until the onion is soft and just beginning to colour (7–8 minutes).
3. Add the cumin, turmeric and chilli powder, and stir-fry for 1 minute. Add the passata or sieved tomatoes, and stir-fry for 2–3 minutes.
4. Add the potatoes and water, bring to the boil and reduce the heat to low. Cover and simmer for 10 minutes.
5. Add the chickpeas (garbanzos) and kasoori methi, then cook until the potatoes are tender (about 5 minutes).
6. Stir in the garam masala and coriander (cilantro) leaves, remove from the heat and serve.

Preparation time: 20–25 minutes
Cooking time: 20 minutes
Serving ideas: Serve with Family Naan (pages 152–4) or Peshawari Naan (pages 155–7).

Aloo Mattar V

(Potatoes with Garden Peas)

Serves 4

Many people do not associate peas with Indian cooking. But, as you will have realised from the recipes in this book, peas are very popular in India. Aloo Mattar is a well-known dish from Northern India. Here I have used new potatoes with peas in a slightly spiced sauce.

3 tablespoons sunflower or corn oil
1 small onion, finely chopped
2 cloves garlic, peeled and crushed
5mm/¼ inch cube root ginger, finely grated
¼ teaspoon ground turmeric
¼–½ teaspoon chilli powder
½ teaspoon dried mint
450g/1lb/3 cups old potatoes, boiled and halved
150ml/5fl oz warm water
100g/4oz/¾ cup frozen garden peas or cooked fresh peas
1 teaspoon salt or to taste
2–3 ripe tomatoes, skinned and chopped
½ teaspoon Garam Masala (pages 22–3)
2 tablespoons chopped coriander (cilantro) leaves

1. In a sauté pan or wok, heat the oil over medium heat and add the onion. Stir-fry for 4–5 minutes or until starting to colour. Reduce the heat if necessary.
2. Add the garlic and ginger, and stir-fry for 1 minute. Add the turmeric and chilli powder. Stir-fry for 1 minute.
3. Add the mint potatoes, water and salt, bring to a slow simmer, cover and cook for 5–6 minutes. Stir in the peas, tomatoes and garam masala. Simmer for 3–4 minutes.
4. Add the coriander (cilantro) leaves and cook for 1 minute. Remove from the heat and serve.

Preparation time: 20–25 minutes
Cooking time: 12–15 minutes
Serving ideas: Serve with Family Naan (pages 152–4) and Tarka Dhal (pages 111–12) or Palak Choley (page 120–1) or Rajma Masala (pages 109–10).

Kashmiri Sabziyon V

(Kashmiri Vegetables)

Serves 4

Kashmir is a fruit-lover's paradise. It is also the only state in India where mushrooms grow naturally.

3 tablespoons sunflower or soya oil
1 small onion, finely chopped
3–4 cloves garlic, peeled and crushed
1cm/½ inch cube root ginger, peeled and finely grated
1½ teaspoons ground coriander
1 teaspoon ground cumin
½ teaspoon ground turmeric
½ teaspoon chilli powder
1 teaspoon paprika
225g/8oz/2 cups closed cup mushrooms, sliced
125g/4oz dried, ready to eat apricots, halved
175g/6oz/¾ cup canned unsweetened pineapple cubes, drained
50g/2oz/⅓ cup glacé cherries, halved and rinsed
1 teaspoon salt
½ teaspoon sugar
¼ teaspoon Garam Masala (pages 22–3)
150ml/5fl oz single cream
1 tablespoon chopped coriander (cilantro) leaves

1. In a karahi, wok or other suitable pan, heat the oil. When hot, add the onion, garlic and ginger. Reduce the heat slightly and fry until the onion is soft (4–5 minutes).
2. Add the ground coriander, cumin, turmeric, chilli powder and paprika. Stir-fry for 1 minute.
3. Add the mushrooms, apricot, pineapple, cherries, salt and sugar. Cover and simmer for 5 minutes.
4. Stir in the garam masala and cream. Cover and simmer for a further 5 minutes.
5. Add the coriander (cilantro) leaves, remove from the heat and serve.

Preparation time: 15 minutes
Cooking time: 12-15 minutes
Serving ideas: Serve with Kashmir ki Roti (pages 150–1) and Dhal Panchrattan (pages 107–8).

Rice and Bread

In this chapter, I have provided a selection of bread which can be made ahead of time and frozen, so you can serve your meals at supersonic speed. As an easy alternative, for mid-week meals, shop-bought Indian breads can make life easier. Wholemeal pitta bread, warmed under the grill with a little butter spread on, is an excellent time saver. Chapatties, naans etc. are sold in most supermarkets these days. You can also combine bread and rice as is done for traditional Indian meals. To make your meals varied, interesting and more balanced, I have included a selection of rice recipes. Details of preparing and cooking rice can be found on page 8. Rice provides protein, vitamins and minerals and you will have plenty of dietary fibre from the bread. We all know how important fibre is in reducing blood cholesterol.

Sada Chawal

(Plain Boiled Basmati Rice)

Serves 4–6

The wonderful natural aroma and flavour of basmati rice seems to have the power to complement any accompanying dish. In India, basmati is known as 'the king of rice'; it receives a special treatment which no other rice does. Unlike other long-grain rice, basmati is not packed for the market just after it is harvested. It is matured for two to four years before it is ready for commercial purposes. It is during this maturing time that the rice develops that wonderful, distinctive flavour, a bit like good wine! Please read the instructions for preparing and cooking rice before you try this or any other rice recipe in this chapter.

275g/10oz/1½ cups basmati rice
550ml/18 fl oz/2⅓ cups water
½ teaspoon salt
knob of butter

1. Wash the rice in several changes of water and soak for 30 minutes. Drain thoroughly.
2. Put the water in a karahi, wok or saucepan and bring to the boil over high heat. Add the rice, salt and butter, bring back to

the boil and cook for 1 minute. Reduce the heat to low and cover the pan tightly (if using karahi use a piece of foil to cover). Cook for 10 minutes without lifting the lid. Remove from the heat and set aside, undisturbed, for 10–15 minutes.

3. Fork through the rice, and using a flat metal or plastic spoon, transfer it to a serving dish.

Preparation time: A few minutes, plus soaking the rice
Cooking time: 15 minutes
Serving ideas: Serve with any curry.

Kesari Chawal

(Saffron Rice)

Serves 4–6

The best varieties of saffron come from India (Kashmir) and La Mancha in Spain.

275g/10oz/1½ cups basmati rice
600ml/1 pint/2½ cups water
2 x 2.5cm/1 inch pieces cinnamon sticks
6 whole cloves
6 green cardamom, split to the top of each pod
½ teaspoon black peppercorns
2 bay leaves crumbled
1 teaspoon salt
½ teaspoon saffron strands, pounded
2 tablespoons hot milk
50g/2oz/¼ cup ghee or unsalted butter (page 21)
1 large onion (about 250g/8oz/2 cups), finely sliced

To garnish

15g/½oz toasted flaked almonds
few sprigs of fresh coriander (cilantro) leaves

1. Wash the rice in several changes of water and soak for 15–20 minutes. Drain well.
2. Put the water, cinnamon, cloves, cardamom, peppercorns, bay leaves and salt into a saucepan. Bring to the boil, cover and simmer for 15 minutes. Strain and set aside.
3. Soak the saffron in the hot milk and set aside for 10–15 minutes.
4. Melt the ghee over medium heat in a heavy saucepan. Add the onion and stir-fry until a pale golden colour, about 9–10 minutes. Add the rice, reduce the heat to low and stir-fry for 2–3 minutes.
5. Add the spiced liquid and saffron milk with all the strands and increase the heat to high. Bring to the boil, cover the pan and reduce the heat to very low. Cook for 10 minutes. Remove from the heat and leave undisturbed for 10–15 minutes.
6. Fork through the rice, then using a flat plastic or metal spoon, transfer to a serving dish. Serve garnished with toasted almonds and sprigs of coriander (cilantro).

Preparation time: 15 minutes, plus soaking the rice
Cooking time: 25–30 minutes
Serving ideas: Serve with Paneer Makhani (pages 54–5) and a raita.
Suitable for freezing.

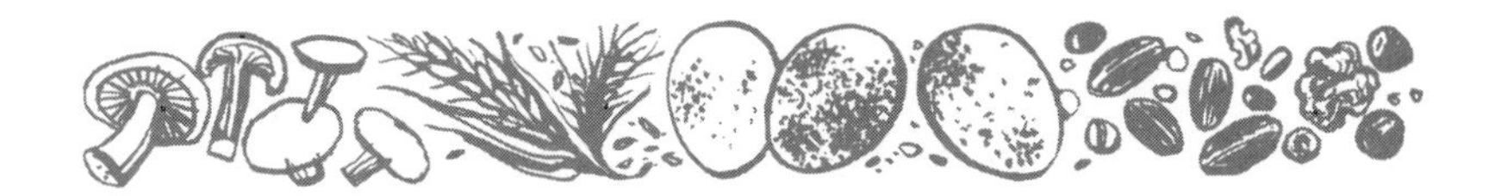

Khumb Pulao

(Mushroom Pulao)

Serves 4–6

The exquisite basmati rice, which grows in abundance in the foothills of the Himalayas, is the natural choice for Pulao (Pilau Rice). You will be delighted with this Mushroom Pulao.

275g/10oz/1½ cups basmati rice
50g/2oz/¼ cup ghee or unsalted butter (page 21)
4 green cardamom pods, split to the top of each pod
2 x 2.5cm/1 inch pieces cinnamon sticks
2 bay leaves, crumbled
4 cloves garlic, peeled and crushed
4 whole cloves
1 large onion (about 225g/8oz/2 cups), finely sliced
1 green chilli, seeded and chopped
1 teaspoon Garam Masala (pages 22–3)
75g/3oz/⅓ cup canned chopped tomatoes including juice
225g/8oz/⅓ cup large flat mushrooms, cut into chunky pieces
2 tablespoons chopped coriander (cilantro) leaves
1 teaspoon salt or to taste
550ml/18 fl oz/2⅓ cup warm water

1. Wash the rice in several changes of water and soak for 15–20 minutes. Drain and set aside.
2. Place a heavy-based saucepan over low heat, then add the ghee or butter. When melted, add the cardamom, cinnamon and bay leaves, and let them sizzle for 15–20 seconds.
3. Add the garlic and cloves, and stir-fry for 30 seconds, then add the onion and chilli. Increase the heat to medium and stir-fry for 6–7 minutes or until lightly browned.
4. Add the garam masala and stir-fry for 30 seconds. Add the tomatoes and stir-fry for 1 minute.
5. Add the rice, mushrooms, coriander (cilantro) leaves and salt, stir-fry for 1 minute, then add the water. Bring to the boil, and cook for 1 minute. Reduce the heat to low, cover the pan with a piece of foil or a lid and cook for 10 minutes. Remove from the heat and leave to stand undisturbed for 6–8 minutes. Remove the whole spices if desired, and fork through the pulao before serving.

Preparation time: 20 minutes, plus soaking the rice
Cooking time: 25 minutes
Serving ideas: Serve with Tarka Dhal (pages 111–12) and a raita.
Suitable for freezing.

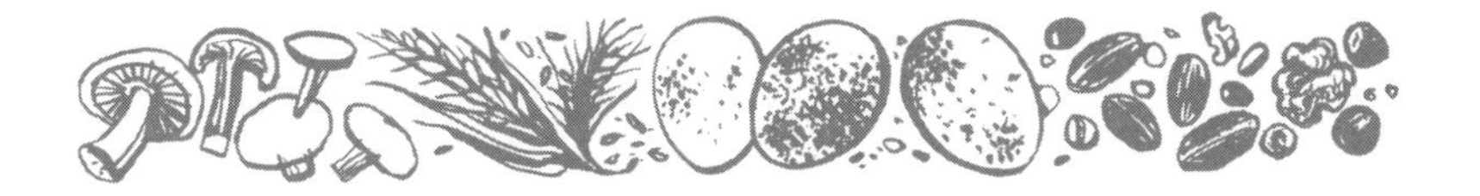

Kashmiri Sabzi Pulao

(Kashmiri Vegetable Pulao)

Serves 4

A few centuries ago, the 'Naga' tribes of Kashmir were ruled by Kashya, a good and benevolent leader. As a tribute to him, his people named this land 'Kashya-Mor' which means 'Abode of the descendants of Kashya'. 'Kashya-Mor' became 'Kashmir'. The 'Sarawat' tribes eventually forced the Nagas to migrate from this region.

Kashmir is renowned for its exotic fruits and vegetables which the local people have used very imaginatively to create wonderful dishes.

175g/6oz/2 cups large flat mushrooms
40g/1½oz/¼ cup ghee or unsalted butter (page 21)
1 onion (about 175g/6oz/1½ cups), finely sliced
2–3 x 2.5cm/1 inch cinnamon sticks
4 whole cloves
4 green cardamom pods, split to the top of each pod
2 bay leaves, crumbled
50g/2oz/⅓ cup dried, ready-to-eat apricots, sliced
75g/3oz/¼ cup canned pineapple cubes, well drained
50g/2oz/⅓ cup glacé cherries, halved and rinsed

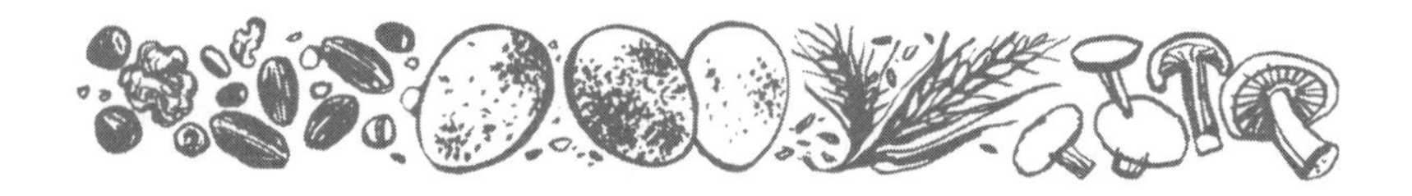

225g/8oz/1¼ cups basmati rice, washed, soaked in cold water for 30 minutes, well drained
1 teaspoon salt or to taste
½ teaspoon chilli powder
475ml/16 fl oz/2¼ cups warm water
1 tablespoon chopped coriander (cilantro) leaves

1. Quarter the mushrooms and halve each quarter.
2. In a heavy saucepan, melt the ghee or butter, and when hot but not smoking, add the onion, cinnamon, cloves, cardamom and bay leaves. Stir-fry for 3–4 minutes. Over medium heat, reduce the heat slightly and continue to fry until the onions are brown.
3. Add the mushrooms and stir-fry for 2 minutes.
4. Add all the fruits, with the rice, salt and chilli powder, and stir-fry for 2–3 minutes, over low heat.
5. Add the water, bring to the boil and cook for 5 minutes. Add the coriander (cilantro) leaves and stir well.
6. Reduce the heat to very low, cover the pan tightly and cook for 6–7 minutes. Remove from the heat and leave to rest for 5–7 minutes. Use a metal or thin plastic spatula to stir and serve the rice, a wooden spoon will squash the grains.

Preparation time: 10–15 minutes, plus soaking the rice
Cooking time: 25 minutes
Serving ideas: Serve with Dhal Makhani (pages 113–14) and Tamatar aur Khira ka Raita (pages 171–2).
Suitable for freezing.

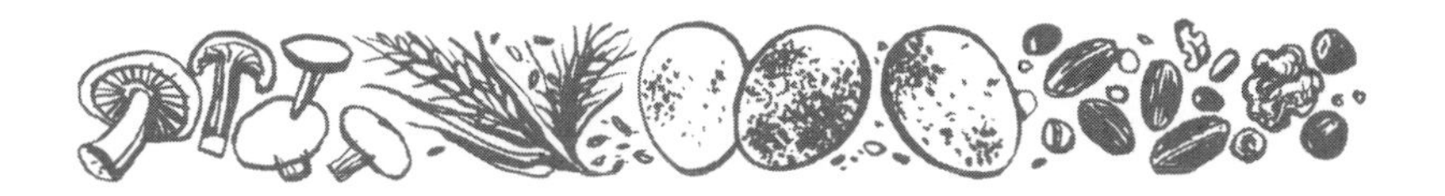

Kashmir ki Roti

(Kashmiri Bread)

Makes 8

Barley and wheat have been staple foods of the Himalayan region since the Harappan times. Archaeological findings include brick built objects with remains of wooden pestles to grind wheat into flour. Kashmiris still follow this practice today. The modern day tava (iron griddle) for cooking bread, must have been refined to its present state from clay and metal plate models found in the Indus Valley sites.

450g/1lb/3¼ cups atta or chapatti flour
1 teaspoon salt
2 teaspoons sugar
1 teaspoon shahi jeera (royal cumin)
1 teaspoon onion seeds (kalonji)
275ml/8 fl oz/1¼ cups warm milk
50g/2oz/¼ cup ghee or unsalted butter, melted (page 21)
Oil for shallow frying

1. Put the flour, salt, sugar, shahi jeera and kalonji in a large mixing bowl and mix thoroughly.

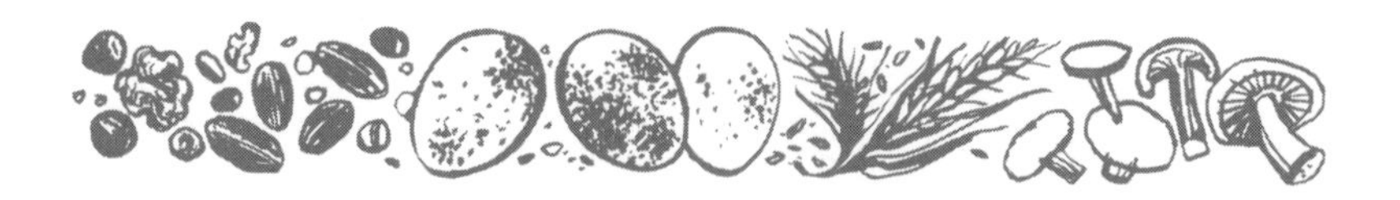

2. Gradually add the warm milk and knead until a dough is formed. Alternatively, use a food processor with a dough hook. For both methods, now add the melted ghee or butter and knead for 2–3 minutes or until the fat is absorbed by the dough. If using a food processor, knead the dough until it stops sticking to the bowl and dough hook. For the hand method, transfer the dough to a pastry board and knead until it is soft and pliable and stops sticking to the board. Divide the dough into 2 equal parts and make 4 equal portions out of each. Rotate each portion between your palms to make a ball, then flatten by pressing down. Cover the flattened cakes with a damp cloth and set aside for 20 minutes.
3. Preheat a cast iron griddle or other heavy-based frying pan over medium heat. Roll out a flattened cake to a 20.5cm/8 inch round disc and place on the griddle. Allow to cook for 1 minute, turn over and cook the other side for 1 minute. Meanwhile, spread a little oil (about 1 teaspoon) on the cooked side, turn over and spread oil on the second cooked side. Cook the first oiled side until brown patches appear; you can check this by lifting the roti gently. Turn it over and cook the second oiled side.
4. Place the cooked roti on one end of a long piece of foil lined with absorbent paper. Cover with the other end to keep hot while you cook the remaining rotis.

Preparation time: 15–20 minutes
Cooking time: 20–25 minutes
Serving ideas: Serve with Moong Dhal Jhal Frazi (pages 115–16).
Suitable for freezing.

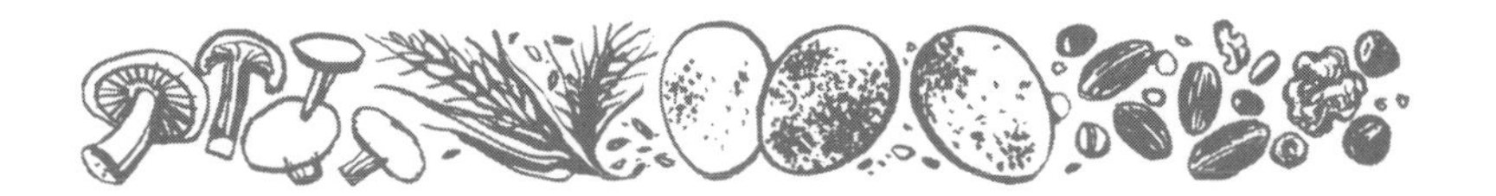

Family Naan

Makes 3

Kabul, the capital of Afghanistan, boasts the greatest and the best variety of naans. It must have been from Afghanistan that the Pathans first took naan to the North West Frontier Province. There is nothing really different about Family Naan except its size. It can be as long as 45.5cm/18 inches and as wide as 25.5cm/10 inches! I first came across this size in a frontier restaurant during a visit to New Delhi.

450g/1lb/3¼ cups plain flour
1½ teaspoons baking powder
1 teaspoon salt
1 tablespoon sugar
1 teaspoon onion seeds (kalonji)
1 teaspoon shahi jeera (royal cumin)
50g/2oz/¼ cup ghee or unsalted butter, melted (page 21)
275ml/8 fl oz/¼ cup warm milk
40g/1½oz natural yogurt

1. Put the flour, baking powder, salt, sugar, onion seeds and shahi jeera in a large mixing bowl and mix well. Add the

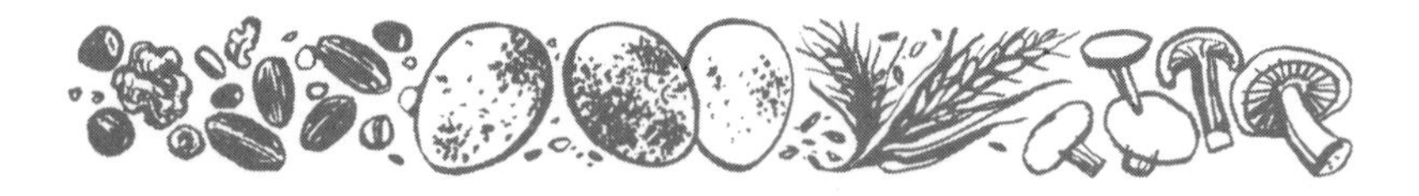

ghee or butter and work it in with your fingertips. Alternatively, use a food processor with a dough hook and mix for a few seconds. The next step applies to both methods.

2. Gradually add the milk and mix until a soft dough is formed. For the hand method, transfer the dough to a pastry board and knead for 3–4 minutes until the dough is soft and smooth and does not stick to your fingers any more. If using a food processor, run it until all the milk is absorbed, then stop the processor and feel the dough. The dough hook and sides of the bowl should be clean, and the dough should feel soft and smooth. Put the dough in a plastic food bag or cover it well, and allow to rest for 1–1½ hours.
3. Preheat the oven to 220°C/425°F/gas mark 7. Preheat a large baking sheet and place greased greaseproof paper or baking parchment on top.
4. Use a large pastry board or flat surface to roll out the naan. Grease the board and the rolling pin lightly. Divide the dough into 3 equal parts, then make a smooth round ball. Flatten the ball and roll out to a 20cm/8 inch disc. Gently pull the lower end to form a teardrop shape, and roll again to make it about 40.5cm/16 inches long, main-taining the teardrop shape. The widest part can be about 23cm/9 inches and the narrowest 10cm/4 inches.
5. It is not necessary for you to make the naan into a teardrop shape. You can make them round or square if you like. This traditional shape is due to the fact that naan is hung onto the wall of the tandoor, the Indian clay oven. Gravity causes the naan to stretch, thus forming a teardrop shape.

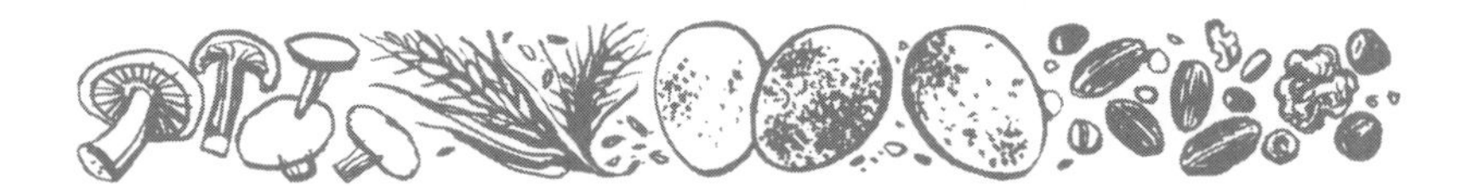

6. Place the naan on the prepared baking sheet and brush generously with the natural yogurt. Bake on the top shelf of the oven for 8–9 minutes. Until you finish baking all 3 naan, keep baked ones warm by wrapping in foil lined with absorbent paper.

Preparation time: 10–15 minutes, plus resting the dough
Cooking time: 25–28 minutes
Serving ideas: Serve with any Indian dish.
Suitable for freezing.

Peshawari Naan

Makes 6

Peshawar, in the North West Frontier Province close to the Khyber Pass, is a 'Pathan' stronghold. The Pathans, believed to be originally from Israel, made their first home in Afghanistan. It was here that they were converted to Islam. Today they are found living in various towns and cities in northern India and Pakistan. Peshawari Naan needs no introduction! It must be the most popular bread that forms part of most Indian restaurant menus. Here is my version.

450g/1lb/3¼ cups plain flour
1 teaspoon baking powder
1 teaspoon salt
1 tablespoon sugar
1 dessertspoon easy-blend (instant) yeast
160g/5½oz/⅔ cup ghee or unsalted butter, melted (page 21)
290ml/9 fl oz/1⅓ cups warm milk
15g/½oz seedless raisins, coarsely chopped
25g/1oz/⅓ cup flaked almonds, lightly crushed
little extra flour for dusting
1 tablespoon natural yogurt
1 tablespoon white poppy seeds or sesame seeds

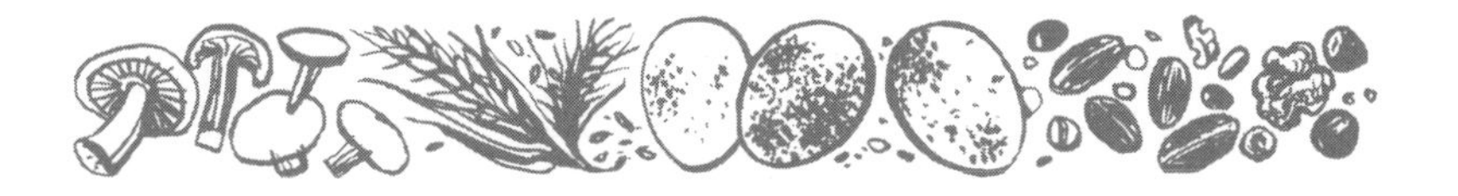

1. Put the flour, baking powder, salt, sugar and yeast in a large warmed mixing bowl and mix thoroughly. Add half the melted ghee or butter and mix well. Gradually add the warm milk and mix into a stiff dough. Alternatively, use a food processor with a dough hook.
2. For both methods, now add the remaining melted ghee or butter and knead for 2–3 minutes for the hand method, and 50–60 seconds in the food processor. The dough will be very sticky at this stage – do not panic!
3. For the hand method, transfer the dough onto a pastry board, add the raisins and almonds, and knead until it stops sticking to the board and your fingers. Make sure the raisins and almonds are well distributed. If using a food processor, add the raisins and nuts and run it until the bowl and the dough hook are clean.
4. Put the dough in a large plastic bag and tie securely, leaving room for expansion. Put the bag in a warmed bowl, preferably a steel one as it will retain the heat better. If you do not have one, use a saucepan. Leave in a warm place (the airing cupboard is ideal) for 1–1½ hours to prove.
5. Divide the dough into 2 parts and make 3 equal portions from each. Rotate each portion between your palms, and press gently to flatten it into a round cake. Cover the flattened cakes and keep aside for 10 minutes. Preheat the oven to 220°C/425°F/gas mark 7.
6. Lightly dust each cake in flour and roll out to a 15cm/6 inch disc. Place one hand on the top end of the disc and gently pull the lower end to form a teardrop shape. This shape is not absolutely necessary. You can make your naan round or even square if you like!

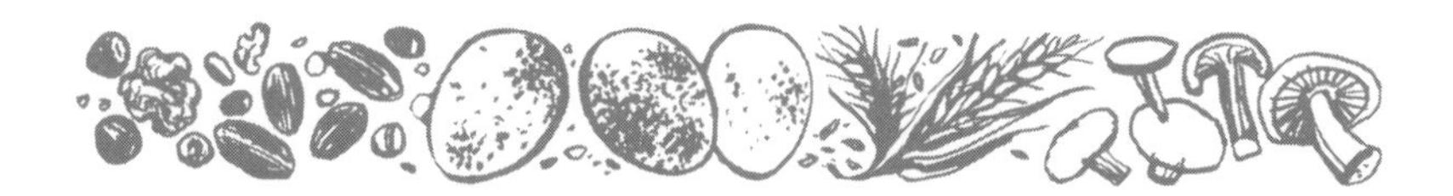

7. Preheat a baking sheet and place greased greaseproof paper or baking parchment on top. Put 2–3 naans on the baking sheet (depending on size), and brush the tops with a little yogurt. Sprinkle with poppy or sesame seeds and bake on the top shelf of the oven for 8–9 minutes or until puffed and lightly browned.

Preparation time: 15–20 minutes, plus proving the dough
Cooking time: 18–20 minutes
Serving ideas: Serve with Aloo Choley (pages 132–3) and a raita.
Suitable for freezing.

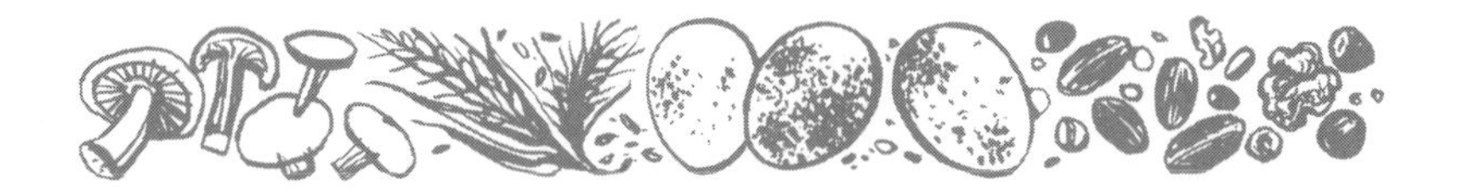

Methi ki Roti V

(Fenugreek-flavoured Bread)

Makes 8

Kasoori methi (dried fenugreek leaves) is an ingredient that gives a distinctive flavour to any dishes. It grows abundantly in Kasoor, in Pakistan – hence the name Kasoori methi – and is considered to be the best. The fresh leaves are dried and chopped with their stalks, which you need to remove. They come in packets and are available in Asian stores.

450g/1lb/3¼ cups atta or chapatti flour
1 teaspoon salt
2 teaspoons sugar
2 tablespoons Kasoori methi, stalks removed
2–3 cloves garlic, peeled and crushed
75ml/3 fl oz/⅓ cup sunflower or corn oil
290ml/9 fl oz/1 cup warm water
extra flour for dusting
Sunflower or corn oil for frying

1. Put the flour in a large mixing bowl. Add the salt, sugar, Kasoori methi and garlic, and mix thoroughly with your fingertips.

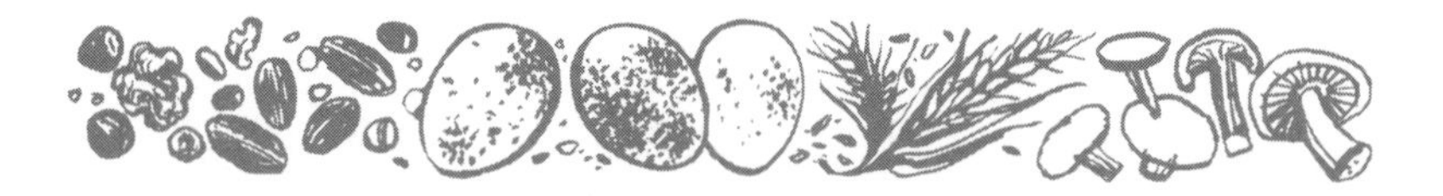

2. Add the oil and work it well into the flour. Gradually add the warm water and knead until you have a soft dough. Transfer the dough to a pastry board and knead with your hands until the dough is soft and smooth and does not stick to your fingers or the board. Alternatively, make the dough in a food processor, kneading the dough until it has stopped sticking to the dough hook and bowl. Now cover the dough with a damp cloth and leave to rest for 20–30 minutes.
3. Divide the dough into 2 equal parts and either break off or cut 4 equal portions from each. Flatten each portion by rotating it between your palms and pressing it down to a flat cake. Cover again with a damp cloth. Preheat a cast iron griddle or other heavy-based frying pan over a medium heat for 2–3 minutes.
4. Dust one flat cake in flour and roll out to an 18cm/7 inch disc. Carefully lift from the board and place on the griddle. Cook for 1 minute, then turn over and cook the other side for 30–40 seconds. Meanwhile, spread the entire surface of the side you cooked first, with 1 teaspoon oil. Turn over the roti and cook until brown patches appear (you can lift it to check this, using a thin flat spatula). Now oil the second side, turn over and cook. Each roti will take 2–3 minutes.Transfer the cooked rotis to a plate lined with absorbent paper.

Preparation time: 15–20 minutes
Cooking time: 25 minutes
Serving ideas: Serve with Makki Khumb Jhal Frazi (pages 97–8) and Rajma Masala (pages 109–10) and a raita or chutney.
Suitable for freezing.

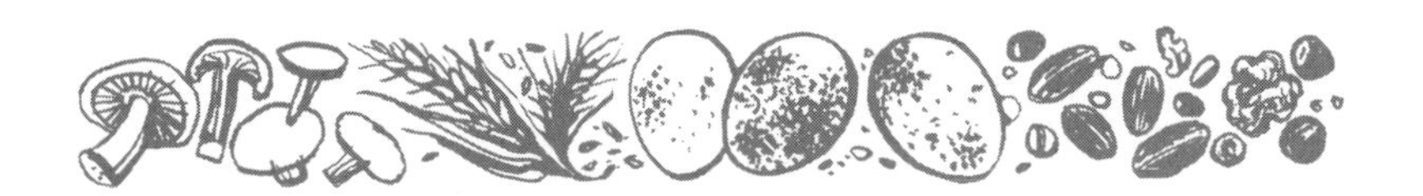

Soda Naan

Makes 6

'Naan' is a Persian word which simply means 'bread'. The Persians, having entered India through the Khyber Pass, first settled in Kashmir. Originally a predominantly Hindu state, it now has a staggering 90 per cent Muslim population. Clay ovens, looking remarkably like the tandoor in which naan is baked, have been found by archaeologists in the Indus Valley Sites.

I offer you this plain naan for which I use soda water in the dough, a tip given by an aunt. This makes the naan wonderfully soft and fluffy: it literally melts in the mouth!

450g/1lb/3¼ cups self-raising flour or plain flour with ½ teaspoon baking powder
1 teaspoon salt
1 teaspoon sugar
1 dessertspoon easy-blend (instant) yeast
65g/2½oz ghee or unsalted butter, melted (page 21)
300–350ml/10–12 fl oz/1⅓–1½ cups soda water

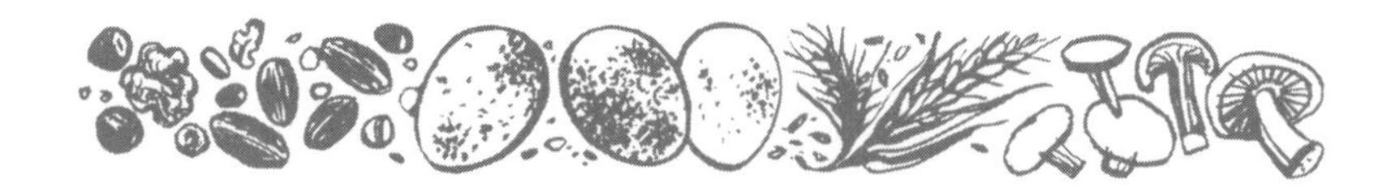

1. Put the flour, salt, sugar and yeast into a warmed bowl and mix thoroughly. (It is best to use flour which is already at warm room temperature.)
2. Make sure the ghee or butter is lukewarm, reserve 1 tablespoon and work the remainder into the flour with your fingertips.
3. Gradually add the soda water and mix until you have a fairly sticky dough. You can make the dough in a food processor with a dough hook if you wish. When the dough is formed, add the reserved fat and knead until the dough does not stick to the bowl or the dough hook.
4. For the hand-mixed method, transfer the dough to a pastry board and knead with your hands for 2–3 minutes. Add the remaining ghee or butter, and knead until the dough stops sticking to your fingers and the board.
5. Put the dough into a large plastic food bag and tie loosely. Place the bag in a warmed metal or steel bowl, or if you do not have one, use a saucepan. Leave the dough in a warm place for 45–50 minutes.
6. Knock back the dough and divide into 4 equal portions, cover and leave to rise again for 15–20 minutes.
7. Preheat oven to 220°C/425°F/gas mark 7. Place greased greaseproof paper or baking parchment on top of a baking sheet.
8. Use a large pastry board or flat surface to roll out the naan. Lightly grease your palms with a little oil then grease a portion of dough by patting and tossing it from one palm to another. Roll out to a 15cm/6 inch disc, and gently pull one end to form a teardrop shape. The shape of the naan is not important. You can make them round or square if you like!
9. Bake on the top shelf of the oven for 8–9 minutes.

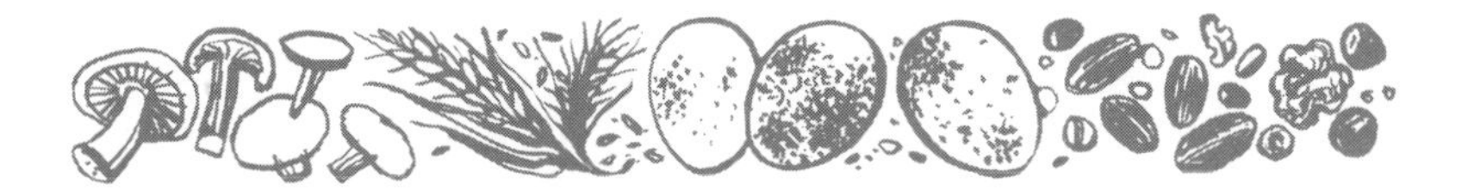

Preparation time: 15–20 minutes, plus proving the dough
Cooking time: 18–20 minutes
Serving ideas: Serve with any curry.

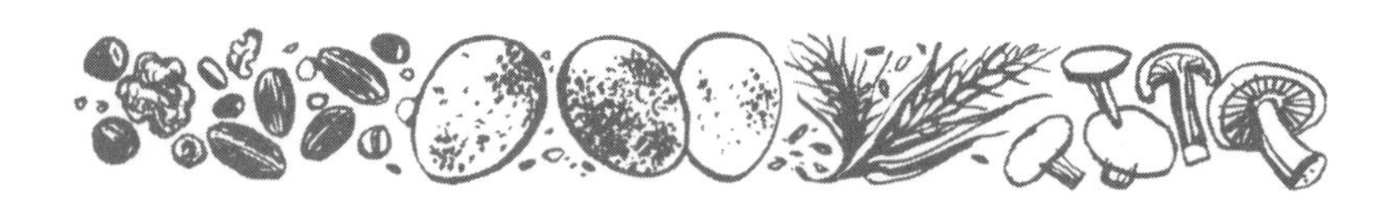

Raitas and Relishes

Raitas and relishes are an integral part of any Indian meal. They add that extra zest to spicy meals and make the entire meal much more interesting.

Traditionally, mild, creamy yogurt is used for raitas. Whole milk natural set yogurts are ideal as is Greek yogurt.

Yogurt is excellent for fighting bacteria related to gastro-intestinal problems. It is wholesome, versatile and very easy to digest.

Ghia ki Chutney

(Courgette (Zucchini) Chutney)

Serves 4–6

The combination of courgette (zucchini) and coconut is wonderful. Traditionally, tender marrow is used in this chutney.

50g/2oz/⅔ cup desiccated coconut
225g/8oz/2 cups courgettes (zucchini), roughly chopped
300ml/½ pint/1⅓ cups water
½ teaspoon salt or to taste
1 teaspoon tamarind concentrate or 1 tablespoon lime juice
1 green chilli, seeded and chopped
1cm/½ inch cube root ginger, peeled and roughly chopped
1 small clove garlic, peeled
15g/½oz/¼ cup coriander (cilantro) leaves, including tender stalks

1. Put the coconut, courgettes (zucchini) and water in a karahi, wok or saucepan and place over high heat. Bring to the boil, reduce the heat to low, cover and simmer for 5 minutes. Add the salt and tamarind, and stir until the tamarind is dissolved. Remove from the heat and allow to cool.

2. Purée the courgette (zucchini) mixture with the remaining ingredients in a food processor until smooth. If using lime juice, add this while blending.

Preparation time: 5 minutes
Cooking time: 6–8 minutes
Serving ideas: Serve with Shakahari Shamee Kabab (pages 30–1), Shakurkandi Pakoras (pages 45–6) or Palak Pakoras (pages 41–2).
Suitable for freezing.

Ghia ka Raita

(Courgette (Zucchini) Raita)

Serves 4

Raitas, pickles and chutneys make Indian meals more appetizing. Raitas are very easy to make and any vegetable can be used for them. I love courgettes (zucchini) or tender marrow stir-fried with garlic before mixing with natural yogurt. I have flavoured this raita with roasted cumin seeds.

1 teaspoon cumin seeds
½ teaspoon black peppercorns
1 tablespoon sunflower or corn oil
2 small or 1 large clove garlic, peeled and crushed
225g/8oz/2 cups courgettes (zucchini), cut into bite-sized pieces
½ teaspoon salt or to taste
150g/5oz/⅔ cup thick set whole milk natural yogurt

1. Preheat a cast-iron griddle or a heavy-based frying pan over medium heat. When hot, dry roast the cumin seeds and peppercorns for 1–2 minutes or until the spices release their aroma. Remove from the pan and allow to cool thoroughly, then crush with a mortar and pestle.

2. Preheat a karahi or wok over medium heat for 1–2 minutes, then add the oil. When hot but not smoking, stir-fry the garlic until lightly browned.
3. Add the courgettes (zucchini) and salt and stir-fry for 2 minutes. Remove from the heat and allow to cool thoroughly.
4. Put the yogurt in a medium mixing bowl and beat with a fork until smooth. Add the courgettes (zucchini) and half the crushed spices. Chill until required. Serve sprinkled with remaining crushed spices.

Preparation time: 10 minutes
Cooking time: 5–6 minutes

Mooli aur Gajjar Ka Raita

(Radish and Carrot Raita)

Serves 4–6

Mooli (white radish) is becoming increasingly available in supermarkets. Combined with carrots, it makes a lovely relish.

100g/4oz/½ cup thick set whole milk natural yogurt
1 teaspoon salt or to taste
1 teaspoon sugar
1 teaspoon bottled mint sauce
½ red onion (about 50g/2oz/½ cup), finely chopped
1 mooli (about 225g/8oz/2 cups), grated
2 carrots (about 200g/7oz/1¼ cups) grated

1. Beat the yogurt with a fork until smooth. Add the salt, sugar, mint and onion and mix thoroughly.
2. Stir in the grated mooli and carrots, mix and chill.

Preparation time: 15 minutes
Cooking time: Nil
Serving ideas: Serve with any curry accompanied by naan or rice.
Variation: Use white cabbage instead of mooli.

Tamatar aur Khira ka Raita

(Tomato and Cucumber Raita)

Serves 4–6

Raita is an important part of an Indian meal and it is enjoyed by vegetarians and meat eaters alike. Plain yogurt, seasoned in a variety of ways, is the basis of any raita. Yogurt has been consumed in India from ancient times. Besides being wholesome and versatile, it is also easy on the digestive system.

150g/5oz/¾ cup thick set whole milk natural yogurt
½ teaspoon salt
1 teaspoon sugar
2 firm ripe tomatoes (about 150g/5oz/¾ cup), seeded and chopped
small piece of cucumber (about 150g/5oz/1 cup), chopped
2 tablespoons finely chopped red onion
1 tablespoon finely chopped coriander (cilantro) leaves
2 teaspoons sunflower or corn oil
½ teaspoon black mustard seeds
6–8 curry leaves

1. Put the yogurt in a mixing bowl and add the salt and sugar. Beat until smooth.

2. Add the tomatoes, cucumber, onion and coriander (cilantro) leaves and mix thoroughly.
3. Preheat a karahi or wok over medium heat for 1–2 minutes and add the oil. When hot but not smoking, add the mustard seeds and curry leaves. As soon as the mustard seeds pop, remove the pan from heat and pour the entire contents over the raita. Stir and mix, chill before serving.

Preparation time: 15 minutes
Cooking time: 2–3 minutes
Serving ideas: Serve with any curry.

Pudina aur Hara Dhaniya ki Chutney

(Mint and Coriander (Cilantro) Dip)

Serves 4–6

Mint is used extensively in Northern India. Kashmir has lovely floating gardens where mint is grown in abundance. If you cannot find fresh mint use bottled mint sauce and omit the lime juice.

15g/½oz/¼ cup mint
15g/½oz/¼ cup (cilantro) coriander leaves
1 tablespoon coarsely chopped red onion
1 green chilli, seeded and chopped
2 small cloves garlic, peeled and chopped
½ teaspoon salt
1 teaspoon sugar
100g/4oz/½ cup thick set whole milk natural yogurt
25g/1oz/⅓ cup ground almonds
1 tablespoon lime juice

1. Remove the mature stalks from the mint and coriander (cilantro). Leave the tender ones on, wash and chop them roughly.
2. Put all the ingredients into a blender and purée until smooth. Chill for 2–3 hours before serving.

Preparation time: 10 minutes
Cooking time: Nil
Serving ideas: Serve with any deep-fried dishes and/or grilled or fried pappodums.

Sweets, Desserts and Drinks

Many recipes in this section consists of those I enjoyed while growing up in Northern and north-Eastern India.

I have used fruits and other ingredients characteristic of these regions to create some new recipes. The dairy products used in these recipes will provide you with plenty of protein and essential minerals. The majority of these dishes are straightforward and simple.

Gulab Jamoon

(Dried Milk Balls in Syrup)

Makes 16

A well-known and much loved sweetmeat from Northern India, Gulab Jamoon is traditionally made with 'khoya' and 'chenna'. Both of these are dairy products which can be made at home, but khoya is quite time consuming. An easy alternative is to use full cream dried milk powder which you can buy from Asian shops. I have simplified it further by using dried skimmed milk powder which is easily obtainable, and to make up the richness, added single cream to the dried milk. The jamoons are cooked twice – first in hot oil and then, immediately, in boiling sugar syrup. This operation needs to be carried out simultaneously, but don't worry it is not as bad as it may sound! Serve the jamoons at room temperature with tea or coffee or chilled with a little whipped cream as a dessert.

175g/6oz/1 cup dried skimmed milk powder
75g/3oz/½ cup fine semolina
1 teaspoon ground cardamom
1 teaspoon baking powder
40g/1½oz/¼ cup ghee or unsalted butter, melted
150ml/¼ pint/⅔ cup single cream

25g/1oz/¼ cup shelled unsalted pistachio nuts, chopped
350g/12oz/1¾ cups granulated sugar
900ml/1½ pints/3¾ cups water
Oil for deep frying
2 tablespoons rose water

1. Put the milk powder, semolina, ground cardamom and baking powder in a large mixing bowl and mix thoroughly. Add the ghee or butter and rub in until blended thoroughly.
2. Add the cream and mix until a soft dough is formed. Knead the dough on a pastry board until smooth. Divide the dough into 2 equal parts and make 8 equal-sized balls from each. Stuff each ball with chopped pistachio nuts and make them as smooth and round as possible without any surface cracks. You can do this by rotating them between your palms.
3. Heat the oil in a karahi or wok over medium heat. At the same time, put the sugar and water in a karahi, wok or saucepan and bring to the boil. Stir until the sugar has dissolved. Turn the heat down to medium-low and simmer while you fry the jamoons.
4. Deep-fry the jamoons in batches in a single layer until they are a rich dark brown colour. When you first put them in the hot oil, they will sink. After 2–3 minutes they will start floating in the oil, if they do not, gently ease them away from the base of the pan using a thin spatula. Turn over once or twice until brown, then remove with a slotted spoon and put straight into the simmering syrup. Cook for 1 minute in the syrup, then transfer to a glass bowl with a slotted spoon. Use 2 glass bowls and put 8 jamoons in each bowl. If you pile them up, they tend to lose their shape.

5. When you have cooked all the jamoons, add the rose water to the remaining syrup. Spoon the rose-flavoured syrup over the jamoons, dividing it equally between the bowls. Let them soak in the syrup for 30 minutes before serving.

Preparation time: 30 minutes
Cooking time: 15–20 minutes

Kesari Annanas

(Saffron-flavoured Pineapple)

Serves 6

Pineapples came to India from South America and in the early days they were found only in the Himalayan region. Today pineapple is a very popular fruit all over India. I have flavoured this lovely fruit with saffron and cinnamon. It makes a wonderfully refreshing way to finish a spicy meal.

1 medium pineapple or 2 x 350g/12oz cans/3½ cups pineapple in syrup
600ml/1 pint/2½ cups water
100g/4 oz/⅔ cup caster (superfine) sugar
3 x 2.5cm/1 inch pieces cinnamon sticks
½ teaspoon saffron strands, pounded
2 teaspoons ground arrowroot
275g/10oz/1⅓ cups unflavoured fromage frais or whipped double cream
375g/13oz can/3⅔ cups guava halves, drained

1. Skin the pineapple and remove the 'eyes' with a small sharp knife. Cut across into 12 slices and remove the hard core with an apple corer. If using canned pineapple, drain and reserve the syrup.

2. Put the water, sugar and cinnamon in a large saucepan and place over a high heat. Bring to the boil, then add the pineapple rings. Cook for 8–10 minutes, and transfer to a large plate with a slotted spoon.
3. Return the saucepan to the heat and add the saffron. Bring to the boil, reduce the heat to medium and cook for 6–7 minutes or until the syrup has reduced to nearly half its original volume. If using canned pineapple, measure 425ml/14 fl oz of the syrup and place over high heat. Add the cinnamon and bring to the boil. Reduce the heat to low and simmer for 5–6 minutes. Add the saffron and simmer for 6–8 minutes. Strain the syrup, return to the saucepan and place over a medium heat. When it begins to bubble, blend the arrowroot with a little water and add to the syrup, stirring. Cook for 2–3 minutes when the syrup will thicken slightly. Remove from the heat and allow to cool.
4. Stack 2 pineapple rings together and place in an individual serving dish. Fill the hollow with fromage frais or cream, spreading about 1 tablespoon on the top but leaving a thin border of pineapple showing. Carefully remove the seeds from guava halves with a teaspoon, then place the guavas on the fromage or cream, hollow side down.
5. Pour on enough saffron-flavoured syrup to cover the pineapple, but not the fromage frais, and chill until required.

Preparation time: 10–25 minutes
Cooking time: 15–20 minutes

Gajjar ka Halwa

(Carrot Fudge)

Serves 4–6

Gajjarka Halwa is a very popular dessert in the northern territories of India and Pakistan. It is made by simmering grated carrots with milk and sugar with a hint of spices. Dried fruits and nuts add a luxurious touch to this dessert.

600ml/1 pint/2½ cups full cream milk
400g/14oz/3 cups carrots, scraped and finely grated
100g/4oz/½ cup caster (superfine) sugar
40g/1½oz/¼ cup ghee
25g/1oz/⅓ cup almonds, blanched and slivered
25g/1oz/¼ cup shelled walnut, broken into bite-sized pieces
25g/1oz/¼ cup seedless raisins
½ teaspoon ground cardamom
½ teaspoon ground nutmeg
2 tablespoons double cream
Whipped double cream to serve

1. Put the milk and carrots in a karahi or wok and bring to the boil over high heat. Reduce the heat to medium, then cook for 15–20 minutes or until the milk evaporates completely. Stir

regularly, scraping up and mixing in any thickened milk that sticks to the sides of the pan. If you do not do this, the milk that is stuck will burn, giving the dessert an unpleasant flavour.

2. Add the sugar and cook, stirring constantly, until the mixture is dry again. Remove from the heat and set aside. If you do not have another karahi, transfer the carrot mixture to a plate. Clean the karahi, place over medium heat and add the ghee. When hot but not smoking, stir-fry the almonds and walnuts until golden brown. Remove with a slotted spoon and drain on absorbent paper.
3. Fry the raisins until they swell up, then drain on absorbent paper. Stir the cardamom and nutmeg into the remaining ghee and immediately follow with the cooked carrot mixture. Stir-fry for 2–3 minutes, then blend in the cream. Reserving a few nuts and raisins, stir the remainder into the carrots. Remove from the heat and transfer to a serving dish. Garnish with the reserved nuts and raisins. Serve hot or cold with a little whipped cream.

Preparation time: 20 minutes
Cooking time: 40–45 minutes

Aam ki Kulfi

(Iced Mango Dessert)

Serves 8

Kulfi is the best known and most popular iced dessert in India. The name 'kulfi' is derived from the conical shaped metal moulds in which it is frozen. Opinions vary as to the origin of kulfi, some believe that it was brought to India by the mighty Moguls from Kabul. Others say that it originated in India after the arrival of the Moguls.

Traditional kulfi moulds are available in some Asian shops, but you can use small plastic containers or decorative individual jelly moulds instead. To give you an idea of the size, traditional moulds hold about two tablespoons of kulfi mix. I often set them in ice lolly moulds too.

375g/13oz/1⅔ cups can evaporated milk
300ml/½ pint/1⅓ cups single cream
1½ tablespoons ground rice
100g/4oz/½ cup granulated sugar
1 teaspoon ground cardamom
450g/1lb/3¼ cups mango purée
25g/1oz/¼ cup shelled unsalted pistachio nuts, roasted and lightly crushed

1. Mix the evaporated milk and single cream together in a heavy-based saucepan and place over medium heat.
2. Mix together the ground rice and sugar, then sprinkle onto the milk mixture, stirring.
3. Continue to stir and cook until the mixture has thickened slightly, this will take 6–8 minutes.
4. Add the ground cardamom, stir and mix thoroughly, and remove from the heat. Allow to cool completely, keeping an eye on the mixture and stirring now and again to prevent a skin forming. When completely cold, stir in the mango purée.
5. Fill small containers of your choice with the mix and put in the freezer for 4–5 hours. Leave at room temperature for 5–6 minutes before removing from the moulds. The texture of kulfi is much harder than that of conventional ice cream.
6. Serve sprinkled with roasted pistachio nuts.

Preparation time: 5 minutes, plus freezing
Cooking time: 10 minutes

Papita aur Anar ki Mithai

(Papaya and Pomegranate Dessert)

Serves 4

The papaya (pawpaw) tree is a common sight in most gardens in the eastern foothills of the Himalayas. I have grown up eating fresh papayas brought down from the tree, they are sweet and juicy, and have a richer reddish pink colour than the ones we see in the shops today. Make sure the papaya is fully ripe before you try this recipe. When ripe, the skin has a yellow tinge and feels slightly soft to the touch. If they feel hard, leave them at room temperature for a couple of days and they will be just right. Pomegranate is sold by good supermarkets. It is excellent for adding that exotic touch, it is the seeds that are eaten and these have to be removed carefully from the fruit.

2 ripe papaya
1 pomegranate
225g/8oz/1 cup unflavoured fromage frais or whipped double cream
1 tablespoon rose water
few mint leaves to decorate

1. Trim both ends of the papaya and cut in half lengthwise. Carefully ease away the seeds with a teaspoon and scrape off the white membrane.
2. Cut the pomegranate in half lengthwise, remove the seeds with a fork, and reserve. If it is really fresh and ripe, you can peel the outer skin like an orange. Remove the white membrane and pith.
3. Mix the fromage frais or cream with the rose water.
4. Line individual serving dishes with some of the reserved pomegranate seeds and place a papaya half in the centre. Fill the hollows with fromage frais or cream. Top with the remaining pomegranate seeds and decorate with mint leaves. Chill for 2–3 hours.

Preparation time: 15–20 minutes
Cooking time: Nil

Phirni

(Ground Rice and Milk Dessert)

Serves 4

This delicious dessert with dried fruits and nuts is flavoured with saffron and rose water with a hint of spices. Traditionally it is chilled and served in earthenware bowls. The addition of evaporated milk is not traditional, but I use it to speed up the cooking process.

½ teaspoon saffron strands, pounded
2 tablespoons very hot milk
15g/½oz ghee
40g/1½oz/¼ cup ground rice
25g/1oz/¼ cup raw cashews, split
25g/1oz/¼ cup seedless raisins
600ml/1 pint/2½ cups milk
300ml/½ pint/1⅓ cups evaporated milk
50g/2oz/¼ cup caster sugar
½ teaspoon ground cardamom
½ teaspoon ground nutmeg
1 tablespoon rose water
50g/2oz/¼ cup dried ready-to-eat apricots, sliced

25g/1oz/¼ cup walnut pieces, lightly browned in a little ghee or butter
15g/½oz/⅛ cup shelled unsalted pistachio nuts, lightly crushed and browned as for walnuts

1. Soak the saffron strands in the hot milk and set aside.
2. Melt the ghee over a low heat in a karahi, wok or heavy-based saucepan, and add the ground rice, cashews and raisins. Stir-fry for 1 minute and add the milk. Increase the heat to high, stir until smoke rises, then reduce the heat and cook for 10–12 minutes or until the mixture thickens slightly, stirring constantly.
3. Add the evaporated milk and sugar, and continue to stir and cook until the mixture resembles the consistency of pouring custard.
4. Add the saffron milk, ground cardamom and nutmeg, stir and cook for 1 minute.
5. Add the rose water, stir and remove from the heat. Stir in half the apricots and allow to cool thoroughly. Stir frequently to prevent a skin forming.
6. Transfer the mixture to a serving dish and chill for 3–4 hours. Top with the remaining apricots and the fried nuts.

Preparation time: 10 minutes
Cooking time: 30–35 minutes

Phalon ka Chaat [V]

(Spiced Fruit Salad)

Serves 4

This is a fabulous combination of exotic fruits which is delicately spiced. Serve it with a cup of Masala Chai (see pages 196–7) for a perfect end to your meal.

2 ripe pomegranates
1 large ripe papaya
1 small or ½ medium pineapple
175g/6oz/1 cup seedless green grapes
175g/6oz/1 cup seedless black grapes
½ teaspoon ground dry ginger
¼ teaspoon freshly milled black pepper
½ teaspoon ground cumin
Pinch of chilli powder
¼ teaspoon dried mint or 6–8 fresh mint leaves, finely chopped
½ teaspoon salt

1. Cut the pomegranates into halves and remove the seeds by peeling off the outer skin like you would peel an orange. If you find this difficult to do, gently ease away the seeds with a fork

and discard the outer skin. Remove white membrane and skin next to the seeds and reserve the seeds.

2. Cut the papaya into half lengthwise and remove the black seeds, scrape off the white membrane you will find under the seeds. Cut the papaya into 2.5cm/1 inch cubes.
3. Peel the pineapple and remove the 'eyes' with a small sharp knife. Remove the central hard core and cut the pineapple into bite sized pieces.
4. Halve the grapes and mix all the prepared fruits in a large mixing bowl. Add the remaining ingredients, except the salt, and mix thoroughly. Chill for 1–2 hours. Stir in the salt and serve.

Preparation time: 25–30 minutes
Cooking time: Nil
Variation: Use a fresh, ripe mango instead of papaya and fresh lychees instead of grapes.

Meethi Lassi

(Sweet Lassi)

Makes 1.1 litres/2 pints

Lassi, sweet or savoury, is a well known and popular drink all over Northern India where the climate can be extreme. The bitter winter is followed by a blazing summer when Lassi is drunk for a cooling effect, on its own or with meals.

450g/1lb/2 cups thick set whole milk natural yogurt
600ml/1 pint/1⅓ cups water
65g/2½oz/⅓ cup caster (superfine) sugar
1 tablespoon rose water
Crushed ice to serve

1. Put all the ingredients except the ice in a blender and blend thoroughly. If you do not have a blender, beat the yogurt until smooth and gradually add the water. Continue to beat until well blended. Add the sugar and rose water and stir until the sugar is dissolved.
2. Pour into tall glasses lined with crushed ice.

Preparation time: A few minutes

Namkeen Lassi

(Savoury Lassi)

Makes 1.1 litres/2 pints

Savoury Lassi, with a touch of spices, served in tall glasses lined with crushed ice, is indeed a welcome sight during the oppressive Indian summer months. Serve any time as a refreshing drink or with meals.

½ teaspoon cumin seeds
½ teaspoon black peppercorns
400g/1lb/2 cups thick set whole milk natural yogurt
12–14 mint leaves
1½ teaspoon salt or to taste
2 teaspoons sugar
600ml/1 pint/1⅓ cups water
Crushed ice to serve

1. Preheat a karahi or other small heavy-based pan over medium heat. Add the cumin and peppercorns, stir and roast until they release their aroma. This will only take a minute or two. Remove from the pan and allow to cool, then crush with a mortar and pestle.

2. Put the crushed spices in a blender and add the yogurt, mint, salt, sugar and half the water. Blend until the mint and spices are thoroughly incorporated. Mix in the remaining water, then pour into tall glasses lined with crushed ice.

Masala Chai

(Spiced Tea)

Serves 4

Masala Chai is very popular in the cold, hilly terrain of India, especially during the winter months. An infusion is made by boiling water and winter spices such as cardamom, cinnamon and cloves and the tea is brewed in this. These spices are known to create body heat and this is another way to keep warm in the bitter climate. Serve Masala Chai after dinner or at any other time as a warming drink.

750ml/1¼ pints/3 cups water
1 x 5cm/2 inch piece cassia bark or cinnamon stick
6 green cardamom pods, split to the top of each pod
4 whole cloves
½ teaspoon fennel seeds
4 teaspoons Assam or Darjeeling leaf tea
Milk and sugar to taste

1. Put the water, cassia or cinnamon, cardamom, cloves and fennel in a saucepan and bring to the boil. Reduce the heat to low, cover and simmer for 5 minutes.

2. Rinse out a teapot with boiling water and add the tea leaves. Strain the spiced liquid into the teapot and brew for 4–5 minutes.
3. Put milk and sugar to taste in individual cups and strain the tea over.

Ananas Ka Masala Sherbet

(Spicy Pineapple Drink)

Serves 6–8

Here is an exotic drink which you can serve chilled on crushed ice during the summer or warmed with a dash of brandy in the winter. You can use cans or cartons of sweetened pineapple juice.

450ml/¾ pint/2 cups water
3 x 2.5cm/1 inch pieces of cinnamon sticks
10 whole cloves
6 brown cardamom pods, bruised
1 litre/1¾ pint/4 cups pineapple juice
175ml/6fl oz/¾ cup malibu
A few mint sprigs

1. Put the water, cinnamon, cloves and cardamom into a saucepan and bring to the boil over high heat. Cover the pan and reduce the heat to low. Simmer for 15–20 minutes. Remove from the heat, allow to cool and strain it.
2. Add the pineapple juice and malibu. Serve in tall glasses lined with crushed ice and garnish with the mint.

Preparation time: 5 minutes
Cooking time: 15–20 minutes

Index